Wha

"John has cut through the modern version of what Christmas has become, to remind us all what the Creator originally intended with his greatest gift of all, his son Jesus. John's book focuses on the truth and hope of what Christmas was intended to be. John's talent as an author is in his sharing of the word of God in a real and authentic way."

—Scott Manjak
former Mayor of Cranbrook, BC
Executive Director of a non-profit social service agency

"John has deep insights and is able to link and draw meaning from events and dates like no one I've ever read. I love the fact that in this book he shows Jesus as a ruler, but not the kind of ruler that we must stay at arm's length from. A must-read for anyone who wants a fresh perspective on the greatest story ever told. Once you read this book, you will have no doubt who the greatest ruler, the greatest gift, of all time is—Jesus."

—Anita Cordell
Film and Commercial Actress

"John Telman's *Christmas Unwrapped* is a charming book centered on the abundant grace of a loving God, something so easily neglected amidst our usual Christmas bustle. Its reflections and narratives are written in an enjoyable and easy-to-read manner, and consistently bring a timely message of hope and encouragement to the reader."

—Bruce Merz
Co-Author of *While He Lay Dying*

"John Telman raises the bar when it comes to providing a tool for friends and family to speak to one another about Jesus and where He fits in their lives. Some family traditions involve going to church only at Christmas and Easter. Some of your friends and co-workers don't know Christmas apart from watching *Miracle on 34th Street* or *It's A Wonderful Life*. *Christmas Unwrapped* is primarily a book about who Jesus is and what His salvation can do in your friend's life, in your co-worker's life, in your spouse's life...in your life. John's book is for anyone, everyone...it is for you."

—Rev. Dave Morton
Minister of a unique five-point regional parish
in the East Kootenays of British Columbia

"John Telman mixes regular anecdotes, famous quotes and scripture to help us avoid Christmas fatigue brought on by materialism and our approach to the season as a 'time of getting.' Rather, he encourages us to build an anticipation of the celebration of Christ's birth as a 'time of meaning.' John cleverly intertwines the prophecies of Christ's birth with the theology of salvation. One warning: you'll have to start reading before *The Night before Christmas. . . .*"

—Dr. Gordon Giesbrecht
Professor of Thermophysiology at the University of Manitoba,
former President of Horizon College and Seminary, and current
Board Chair of Providence University College and Seminary

"A book destined to become a standard for Christmas Bible study. Captivating insights on Christmas which incite one's desire to reach deeper into the fullness of its eternal meaning and purpose. John accomplishes this while sustaining a balanced, practical embrace of treasured cultural and family Christmas traditions."

—Rev. Darrell Alley
Pastor and former Police Officer

Christmas
UNWRAPPED

Christmas
UNWRAPPED

11 INSIGHTS INTO THE DEEPER MEANING OF THE SEASON

JOHN W. TELMAN

CHRISTMAS UNWRAPPED
Copyright © 2017 by John W. Telman

Unless otherwise indicated, all scripture taken from the New American Standard Bible®, Copyright © 1960, 1962, 1963, 1968, 1971, 1972, 1973, 1975, 1977, 1995 by The Lockman Foundation. Used by permission. Scripture marked CEV taken from the Contemporary English Version © 1991, 1992, 1995 by American Bible Society. Used by Permission. Scripture marked KJV taken from the Holy Bible, King James Version, which is in the public domain. Scripture marked NLT taken from the Holy Bible, New Living Translation, copyright ©1996, 2004, 2007 by Tyndale House Foundation. Used by permission of Tyndale House Publishers, Inc., Carol Stream, Illinois 60188. All rights reserved. Scripture marked NIV taken from the Holy Bible, NEW INTERNATIONAL VERSION®. Copyright © 1973, 1978, 1984, 2011 by Biblica, Inc. All rights reserved worldwide. Used by permission. NEW INTERNATIONAL VERSION® and NIV® are registered trademarks of Biblica, Inc. Use of either trademark for the offering of goods or services requires the prior written consent of Biblica US, Inc.

Printed in Canada

ISBN: 978-1-4866-1322-9

Word Alive Press
131 Cordite Road, Winnipeg, MB R3W 1S1
www.wordalivepress.ca

Library and Archives Canada Cataloguing in Publication

Telman, John W., 1959-, author
    Christmas unwrapped : 11 insights into the deeper meaning of the season / John W. Telman.

Issued in print and electronic formats.
ISBN 978-1-4866-1322-9 (paperback).--ISBN 978-1-4866-1323-6 (ebook)

    1. Christmas. 2. Jesus Christ--Nativity. I. Title.

GT4985 T45 2016   394.2663   C2016-903222-1
                                           C2016-903223-X

DEDICATION

To my mother and father, Dorathy and Jacobus Telman.
You made Christmas special for Melody (my sister) and
me as we grew up. I can't imagine Christmas being any
better. Love and the reality of God were so real in our
home. We laughed, we cried…especially when us kids
got what we wanted for Christmas. This book is for you.
I love you both.

—Stoop

CONTENTS

ACKNOWLEDGMENTS

It's a joy to talk about Jesus. He's the reason that we celebrate in December. Although some would rather ignore the connection between Christmas and Jesus, I am grateful to those who give me the opportunity to proclaim Him. Word Alive Press not only encourages my writing but also encourages me to write about Jesus, the subject of my books.

David Morton, Bruce Merz, Anita Cordell, Dr. Gord Giesbrecht, Darrell Alley, and Scott Manjak honored me by reading and endorsing the book. I thank them. Your kind words are so appreciated, and I want you to know that I give thanks to God for friends like you.

Not mentioning my family would be a grave mistake. Carole continues to push and prod me to go deep and to express the truth of Jesus Christ. Not only is she a wonderful wife, she is also an excellent friend to study with. Much of what you will read in this book directly results from talking with Carole.

Thanks go to you, Sharon, for your work on the draft, and to your husband and my friend, Dr. Marc Newman, for the foreword.

I value your words, your ministry, and your help in more ways than you can realize.

Of course, I must also acknowledge my Lord and Savior, Jesus Christ, who not only is the reason for this book but constantly inspires me to consider the wonder and splendor of Christmas.

Foreword

My mom loved Christmas. Every year, for as long as I can remember, shortly after Thanksgiving my mom would begin decorating the house for Christmas. She'd put out the fiberglass "angel's hair," spray "snow" on the windows, set up the nativity scene, and erect the Christmas tree. It felt magical.

Slowly, over the days and weeks, the number of presents would grow under that tree until they resembled an avalanche. Dad would keep looking at the assorted heaps and declare, "Not enough!" We were not a wealthy family, but my folks knew how to handle their money—and it always seemed that each child received some of what they wanted from the Sears Wish Book (except, wisely on our parents' part, that motorcycle...).

When we thought our parents weren't looking, we'd go to the tree and rattle the presents to see if we could figure out what was inside. On Christmas Eve we couldn't sleep. As the youngest boy, I was always sent by my older brothers as the "canary in the coal mine" to see if my parents could be convinced it was time to open presents. This ritual usually began at 4 AM and was repeated on the half-hour until our parents relented.

We'd tumble out of our rooms and scramble to the tree to open the gifts and see what "Santa" had left for us.

Imagine how odd it would've been to run up to the tree and merely admire the beauty of the wrappings, going no further. Wouldn't it seem strange to "ooh" and "ahh" over ribbons and gilt-edged paper, never taking the next step—opening the packages?

About two thousand years ago, God sent us a gift in His Son. The Father sent Him in an interesting package—a tiny baby. Everyone loves babies. They coo and gurgle and laugh. That's what makes Christmas such a popular holiday—the package is so inviting that people come back, year after year, to look at Him. Unfortunately, few ever "open" the present. Some, because of a painful past, feel that the gift is more than they can receive. Others fear that going past the wrapping will require too much.

The Christ Child is the package God sent us at Christmas long ago. But the real present was not merely the child in the manger, but the suffering Savior on the cross who later emerged from the tomb as the Risen Lord. Jesus came not to be an entertaining baby, but to be the Savior of the World.

If you think about it, Christmas without Easter is a hollow, sad story. To celebrate the birth of a child who would die a horrible death at the age of thirty-three would be sadistic were it not for the resurrection. But for those who feel they cannot respond to the free gift of forgiveness through Christ, it's as if the package is never opened. Christmas always extends the promise, but Easter never comes to their lives.

In this book, John Telman opens the Christmas story "package." In doing so, he accomplishes a number of important tasks. First, he takes a well-known story—featured in innumerable picture books, Christmas pageants, and motion pictures—and goes "behind the scenes." When history is represented visually, we can make the mistake of thinking we know more than we do. Tying together Christmas and Easter, Telman presents them as a single gift. He fills in details, both before the birth of Christ and after, adding levels that deepen the understanding of those whose main contacts with Christ are the two major Christian holidays. Jesus isn't merely a baby in a manger who visits once a year. He is "the Lamb of God who takes away the sins of the world."

Second, this isn't a book of lectures designed simply to satisfy the intellectually curious. Instead, in these pages, Telman challenges us to do more than look upon Jesus; we are meant to be drawn to Him, to surrender to Him, and to obey Him so that we might have the great gift of abundant, eternal life which He desires to bestow on His followers.

Finally, Telman explains that although the secular world has embraced Christmas, they have stripped away its true meaning and replaced it with appeals to the senses. In doing so, they think that they are making Christmas accessible to everyone. What they don't realize is that ripping Christ out of Christmas isn't watering down the Gospel, it's replacing it. The Christmas offered by the secular world has no more healing power than any other placebo. It might make people feel good for a while, but it's ultimately empty. And it is unnecessary. Christmas *is* for everyone. *"For God so loved the world, that He gave His only begotten Son, that whoever believes in Him shall not perish, but have eternal life"* (John 3:16).

For all who read these pages, know that Christmas is for you. God has given you a gift. In His Word, He has told you how to open it. The gift is so wonderful that it will completely change your life. Don't be fooled; Jesus did not remain a cute baby lying in the straw. He was, and is, God Incarnate. He grew up, healed many, spoke truth, and through His death and resurrection made a way for a sinful people to be reconciled with Almighty God. This is the Good News. There is a Savior. His name is Jesus.

—Marc Newman, Ph.D.

Dr. Marc Newman is a professor, conference speaker, and commu-nication trainer. He recently retired from teaching in the graduate program at Regent University in order to help pastors communicate more effectively, and to help Christians understand media influence. He is an avid Christmas enthusiast.

Introduction

Christmas, to people like my father—who was born and raised in Amsterdam, Netherlands—consists of significant time in church. To others, Christmas is time with family, getting together with aunts, uncles, cousins and grandparents from far-away places. And, for many, Christmas is nothing special. Family, to them, is a meaningless word. In fact, the season, with all its decorations and songs, is positively irritating to some people.

Christmas comes around every December, and is followed by the celebration of a New Year. The same songs are recycled. Turkey is cooked and eaten. But what is Christmas? To understand just what Christmas is, we would be wise to turn to the one who brought the event into being.

God, the Creator, prophesied that someone would be born who would win a victory over evil that would result in life for all of humankind. Many centuries later, this one, Jesus the Christ, was born. No one else in history is like this man. He was born so that you and I could live—*really* live. I mean more than just physically breathing; I mean to gain a kind of life so abundant that it makes our previous life seem colorless and hollow by comparison. How is this even possible? How could the birth of one child more than two thousand years ago impact our lives today in such a way? And yet it did, and it can.

In this little book, we will see that life—*real* life—is not only possible because of the birth of this baby in Bethlehem—it is yours to take. It's the most amazing story. It's relevant to you and me right now, and for every year hereafter. Reading this book will bring you face-to-face with reality. The one who is the subject of this book actually lived and walked the dusty roads of the Middle East. Since his birth he has impacted lives like no other who has ever lived. He has had more followers than anyone in history. He has been hated by many, and misunderstood by countless more, yet his teaching powerfully influences even the lives of those that don't know him. His name is Jesus. He is called the Christ, the Messiah, the one who would not only show the way to life, but also would give his life as a payment for the sin debt of humanity. His followers suffered persecution and martyrdom because of their love for him. But before he was a man who shook the world, Jesus was born a baby. My desire is for you to know about him and to encounter him in a life-changing way.

Christmas will be transformed into more than cranberries, wrapping paper, multiple trips to the local Wal-Mart, and weight gain when you know Jesus—not just as a baby in a Nativity scene, but as your Lord and Savior. As you read these short chapters, let the truth of who Jesus is deepen your understanding about Christmas.

chapter one

C AND E (CHRISTMAS AND EASTER)

T here are at least two times a year that many think about the Creator—namely, Christmas and Easter. People may even go to a church service. This is not a bad thing, because Christmas and Easter focus on God and his love for all.

I don't usually use the word "Easter," although the title of one of my books is *Easter Unwrapped.* My objection to the word has little to do with any intrinsic meaning. Rather, "Resurrection Sunday" represents better what actually happened 2000 years ago. Billy Graham once told *Time* magazine, "If I were an enemy of Christianity, I would aim right at the Resurrection, because that is the heart of Christianity.[1] The word "resurrection" represents or infers life, and so I tend to avoid using the word "Easter."

When we think of Christmas and Easter, we may think of Santa Claus and the Easter Bunny. However, the truth is that these

---

1   Nancy Gibbs, *Time*, "The Message of Miracles," June 24, 2001. http://content.time.com/time/magazine/article/0,9171,133993,00.html

two characters do not represent the real meaning and intent of Christmas and Easter. At the very foundation of both holidays is the love of God for his creation.

Christmas and Easter are tied together through prophecy. In this chapter, we will look at three such prophecies in particular. But first, we need to understand what prophecy is: the foretelling of an event or a person. Before Jesus was born in Bethlehem, he was prophesied. By contrast, take a look at two other men who are revered by many today. Before Buddha was born, no one knew anything about Buddha. Before Mohammed was born, no one knew anything about Mohammed. But before Jesus was born, over 300 prophecies were given about him. The three prophecies that we will look at were made hundreds of years before his birth, and he fulfilled them all. These prophecies did more than establish his identity—they gave humanity a snapshot of his character and what he would do.

JESUS IS THE ULTIMATE FIGHTER

...I will cause hostility between you and the woman, and between your offspring and her offspring. He will strike your head, and you will strike his heel.

—Genesis 3:15, NLT

UFC (Ultimate Fighting Championship) has nothing on the first prophecy of Jesus Christ, which describes him as a mighty warrior. The Ultimate Fighter, Jesus Christ, will vanquish Satan, who seeks to kill, steal and destroy. Genesis 3:15 is known as the first gospel ("good news"). God gave the first prophecy, and it was to Satan that he told the future. Incidentally, prophecy can either be fore-telling (predicting) or forth-telling (simply declaring the truth of the gospel). In the case of Genesis 3:15, God was simply stating what would happen.

The imagery here is of a snake bruising the heel of the Ultimate Fighter, but ultimately being crushed. That's what happened at Easter: Satan temporarily brought destruction through the crucifixion, but Jesus was raised from the dead and in doing so crushed Satan's head. Satan may make trouble for you and me now, but his demise is certain. We have victory because the Ultimate Fighter prevailed. He won!

The apostle Paul wrote, *"The sting of death is sin, and the power of sin is the law; but thanks be to God, who gives us the victory through our Lord Jesus Christ"* (I Corinthians 15:56-57).

You don't win the ultimate fight of life by keeping all the rules. You won't be able to. The Bible reminds us that we are weak. Even the strongest man, with his bulging muscles, is weak spiritually. Instead of godliness and sinlessness, in our human weakness we all have sinned. But Jesus Christ, the Ultimate Fighter, won the victory—even as God had prophesied many, many centuries before. Remember, God writes history before it happens. This is proof of the truthfulness of God's word.

> . . . *God so loved the world, that He gave His only begotten Son, that whoever believes in Him shall not perish, but have eternal life. For God did not send the Son into the world to judge the world, but that the world might be saved through Him.*

> —John 3:16-17

3

Jesus Christ, the promised one, the Ultimate Fighter, won the victory over sin, hell and the grave! Christmas and Easter are directly connected by God's purpose to give life to you, me and everyone else.

JESUS IS THE MIGHTY RULER

> *...you, O Bethlehem Ephrathah, are only a small village among all the people of Judah. Yet a ruler of Israel, whose origins are in the distant past, will come from you on my behalf.*
>
> —Micah 5:2, NLT

Micah was an eighth-century B.C. prophet. He lived at the same time as the prophets Amos, Hosea and Isaiah. Micah described a wonderful future when the town of Bethlehem would give birth to a ruler greater than King David. The fulfillment of this prophecy can be found in Matthew 2:1-6, Luke 2:4-7 and 15, as well as in John 7:14.

The name "Bethlehem" means "House of Bread." Micah also calls it by another name, "Ephratah" (EFF-ra-tha), which is an older name for the city, and means "Place of Fruitfulness." Bethlehem, the House of Fruitfulness and the House of Bread. How fitting that Jesus should be born in Bethlehem!

The Mighty Ruler, who rules with love and service, was born in this little town rather than in the famous city of Jerusalem. Many leaders rule with manipulation, fear and intimidation, but Jesus rules with loving humility.

Even in the last century, we've become accustomed to rulers who are self-serving and wicked. Hitler, Stalin and Mao were world leaders who destroyed many lives—but Jesus Christ has impacted more lives by ruling with love. His rule creates life and peace.

Jesus still rules in the hearts of his people. We deeply desire to have him as our judge, since he has already paid the penalty for our sin. No one is like him: he is better prepared to rule than anyone else, since he is the one with perfect knowledge of all of us, plus he is perfect love.

He is the Mighty Ruler even now. A pastor or a politician is not the mighty ruler; Jesus is. We trust him with our very lives because of who he is. It's sad, but some people resist his rule and try to make a go of it without him. It's dangerous not to be under the rule of Jesus Christ.

I've heard people say, "We aren't under law. We're under grace." That is partially correct, but partly wrong. We *are* still under law—but a different kind of law.

When we have a relationship with God through Jesus Christ, we are now under the law of the Spirit of life in Christ Jesus. Now we don't lie, because of our love for God and for each other. We don't steal or kill, because of our love for God and man. You see, a relationship with God changes everything.

There is now no condemnation for those who are in Christ Jesus. For the law of the Spirit of life in Christ Jesus has set you free from the law of sin and death. For what the Law could not do, weak as it was through the flesh, God did: sending His own Son in the likeness of sinful flesh and as an offering for sin, He condemned sin in the flesh, so that the requirement of the Law might be fulfilled in us, who do not walk according to the flesh but according to the Spirit.

—Romans 8:1-4

The Mighty Ruler was born that first Christmas, and gave himself for everyone so that we might have life everlasting! No one else has impacted and ruled this world like Jesus Christ has. In fact, history is split into B.C. and A.D. because of him.

JESUS IS THE ONE AND ONLY

. . .the Lord himself will give you the sign. Look! The virgin will conceive a child! She will give birth to a son and will call him Immanuel (which means 'God is with us').

—Isaiah 7:14, NLT

No one in history can compare to Jesus Christ. He's the Ultimate Fighter, the Mighty Ruler, and the One and Only. Like Micah, Isaiah was an eighth-century B.C. prophet. The book of Isaiah is one of the four major prophetic books in the Old Testament, along with Jeremiah, Ezekiel and Daniel.

Chapter 7 of Isaiah was written around 735 B.C. King Ahaz was on the throne, and Isaiah was sent with the message that God was sending a sign, which would be a child called "God is with us" (later, we will further discuss this name). The fulfillment of this prophecy is found in Matthew 1:20-23.

C and E (Christmas and Easter)

God made it very clear that the one who would come to redeem humanity would be unique. No one else would be born of a virgin; no one would represent God's very presence except Jesus Christ.

A psychologist named John Rosen once had a crazy idea about using human presence to help those who were severely mentally handicapped. These patients were totally curled up in their beds, or sat in corners rocking back and forth. No medicine helped.

Dr. Rosen came up with the idea of moving onto the ward of the hospital. He lived there. He got right next to the patients. He was with them and touched them. The amazing thing is that he had great success, and that is exactly what God did when he became present with humankind as the baby Jesus.

The Contemporary English Version (CEV) expresses John 1:14 this way: *"The Word became a human being and lived here with us. We saw his true glory, the glory of the only Son of the Father. From him all the kindness and all the truth of God have come down to us."*

Isn't this amazing? God himself came and lived with us. The verse in its original language (Greek) actually states, idiomatically, that God pitched his tent next to ours. That God himself would lower himself to live not just *with* us, but *in* our very lives, boggles the mind—but that's what he did.

Have you ever decided to sin, but then felt the presence of God strongly in that moment? I have, and felt that God could not only see me but was looking right over my shoulder. God is present, and not just when we sin. He is present at all times. Even when things go wrong, God is still present.

Isaiah prophesied to the wicked king Ahaz that God would really show up, and that he would be born in the most unlikely place.

There are many names applied to Jesus after the introductory phrase "He shall be called," both in the Old and New Testaments. This was a common way of saying that people would refer to Him in various ways. In other cultures, names were used to describe the character of the person. That's not always the case in our Western culture. Jesus Christ is "God with us" (Immanuel). He invites us to walk with him through our lives and find that he is our help in all situations.

Robert Louis Stevenson, the Scottish novelist and poet, wrote, "The body is a house of many windows: there we all sit, showing ourselves and crying on the passers-by to come and love us."[2]

The good news is that God saw and heard our cry, and answered it when the second person of the Trinity was born to a virgin. Jesus Christ is the One and Only. Read the first chapter of Colossians and you will find a complete description of who Jesus really is. The heading of verses 13-29 in the New American Standard Bible is "The Incomparable Christ."

God is not an add-on to our lives. We shouldn't consider him only twice a year. There's too much that we could miss, and this world is dangerous. We need him all year round. Jesus Christ is not a crutch—he's the whole hospital.

There are more than three hundred prophecies about Jesus coming for the first time, but there are over fourteen hundred prophecies telling us that he's coming again. But even before he physically

2   Robert Louis Stevenson. (n.d.). BrainyQuote.com. Retrieved January 11, 2016, from BrainyQuote.com website: http://www.brainyquote.com/quotes/quotes/r/robertloui139234.html

returns to bring peace to his creation, we can experience his victory in our lives right now! He invites us to make him *Lord* of our lives, in, between, and through the C and the E of Christmas and Easter. Let's be people who walk with him throughout the entire year.

chapter two

CHRISTMAS FEAR NOTS

On four occasions leading into the first Christmas, individuals were told to "fear not":

1. The priest Zacharias (Luke 1:13)
2. Joseph (Matthew 1:20)
3. Mary (Luke 1:30)
4. The shepherds (Luke 2:10)

In all four of these scripture passages the word that is used for fear is the Greek word *phobeo,* from which we get our English word *phobia.* 366 times in scripture it is written, "Do not fear"—yet fear is powerfully acted out countless times every day.

Here are a few fears that actually exist:

- Ablutophobia – fear of bathing, washing, or cleaning
- Anthophobia – fear of flowers
- Ecclesiophobia – fear of churches
- Osmophobia, olfactophobia – fear of odors

- Cherophobia – fear of happiness
- Philophobia – fear of love
- Phobophobia – fear of fear itself

Fear may not be the first thing that comes to mind when talking about Christmas, but fear actually motivates much that happens in life. In this chapter, we will see why Zacharias, Joseph, Mary and the shepherds were told not to be afraid.

GOD HEARS

The angel said to him, "Do not be afraid, Zacharias, for your petition has been heard, and your wife Elizabeth will bear you a son, and you will give him the name John. . ."

—Luke 1:13

Zacharias, we are told, was a priest who encountered an angel in the temple. He was terrified, but was told not to fear because God had heard his prayer.

We often pray and don't see an answer, but God does hear! It's vital for us to understand that fear, at its core, is doubt. Doubt is dispelled when we remember that God is all-knowing. Nothing is hidden from him; every tiny detail about you and me is known by God. The Psalmist said, *"You know it all"* (Psalm 139:4). And yet God does not act like a know-it-all. He does not offer solutions without hearing us completely. In fact, at times it may appear that God is not acting on our behalf simply because he understands that, initially, we need someone to listen to how we feel. I know this from experience.

On occasion when my son has told me about a problem he was experiencing, I heard his words, but missed how he was feeling. Too often I made the mistake of giving him advice before really hearing him out. Even when I presented a solution that might have worked, he seemed inconsolable. Perhaps what he really needed first was an ear to hear him.

Isn't God so wonderful? Not only does he have answers, he also has a listening ear, and will hear our heart's cry. Imagine! God, the Creator who sees and knows all, actually listens. He could speak, and he does, but first he listens. What wonderful grace and love he has for all of us.

Have you ever had a conversation with someone who is just waiting to speak? They are waiting for you to stop talking so they can offer their perspective. God, whose wisdom makes all of man's wisdom look ridiculous, is not like that. He is patiently listening.

Zacharias didn't just receive a son in answer to his prayer, he also became the father of John the Baptist, who had the honor of being a forerunner to the Messiah. We need not fear. Instead, we go to God in faith—believing that he is good, he loves, and he hears!

JESUS IS FROM GOD

. . .behold, an angel of the Lord appeared to him in a dream, saying, "Joseph, son of David, do not be afraid to take Mary as your wife; for the Child who has been conceived in her is of the Holy Spirit. . ."
—Matthew 1:20

Like Zacharias, Joseph was told not to fear. Also like Zacharias, Joseph was called a righteous man. If someone is disobedient and rebellious toward God, they have every reason to be afraid—but Joseph was instructed not to be afraid to take Mary as his wife. A righteous man does not put himself in any position that would appear to be immoral, and Joseph was not the father of Jesus, giving him ample cause to call off his engagement to the pregnant Mary. However, the angel told him that the baby was from God rather than the result of human procreation.

Some think that Jesus was just a good teacher. Wrong! He is not like any other man. He is unique, so don't be afraid. Put your trust in him! Trusting in anything outside yourself is scary—but if you give your life to him, you don't need to fear!

There are skeptics, including religious leaders, who don't believe in the virgin birth, but Joseph was told that the baby Mary carried was supernatural. When you doubt God, fear overtakes you. Thus, those who will not accept that Jesus was conceived of the Holy Spirit actually sow the seeds of fear for themselves. But God has not given us a spirit of fear! His gift was Jesus the Messiah—the one who can change our existence from fear and condemnation to life and joy!

A Sunday school was putting on a Christmas pageant which included the story of Mary and Joseph coming to the inn. One boy wanted very much to be Joseph, but when the parts were handed out, a child he didn't like was given that role, and he was assigned to be the innkeeper instead. He was pretty upset about this, but he didn't say anything to the director. During the rehearsals, he pondered what he might do on the night of the performance to get even with this rival who had won the coveted role. Finally, on the night of the performance, Mary and Joseph came walking across the stage. They knocked on the door of the inn, and the innkeeper opened the door and asked them gruffly what they wanted. Joseph answered, "We'd like to have a room for the night." Suddenly the innkeeper threw the door open wide and said, "Great, come on in and I'll give you the best room in the house!" For a few seconds poor little Joseph didn't know what to do. Thinking quickly on his feet, he looked inside the door past the innkeeper and then declared, "No wife of mine is going to stay in a dump like this. Come on, Mary, let's go to the barn." And, once again, the play was back on track!

While we might encounter a cute scene like this at a church Christmas play, the real Joseph had to choose strength and not fear. He was charged with an important role in the Christmas story. Joseph was told not to fear, but this was really an invitation to choose to trust God. Joseph played an important part in that first Christmas. He had to trust what God had said through the angel. Remember: fear is a choice, and so is trust.

GOD GIVES HIS FAVOR

The angel said to her, "Do not be afraid, Mary; for you have found favor with God."

—Luke 1:30

Once again an angel was sent to bring God's message to someone. Mary, a teenage girl, was told twice by an angel that she had found favor with God. One of my favorite Greek words is *charis*. It is the word that we often translate as "grace" in English. The meaning behind the word is that God helps and influences us.

Ephesians 2:8 says that it's by God's *charis*, his grace, that we are saved. Salvation is all from God. Nothing we can do can merit salvation; it's all accomplished by God's help and influence in our lives. This is the same word that has been translated as "favor" in English.

Many have believed that Mary was almost perfect, and that was the reason she was chosen to be the mother of Jesus. Wrong! Mary saw God's help and influence in her life, so she knew not to be afraid! Mary, like us, needed God's help. She had sinned, as all people do, but she put her trust in God.

Look at what Mary said:

> ...*my soul praises the Lord. How my spirit rejoices in God my Savior! For he took notice of his lowly servant girl, and from now on all generations will call me blessed. For the Mighty One is holy, and he has done great things for me. He shows mercy from generation to generation to all who fear him.*

—Luke 1:46-50, NLT

Mary was unique not because she was perfect, but because she trusted in God. Therefore, when the angel spoke to her, she was told not to be afraid; she had received God's influence and help. This grace came not as a reward, but because she simply trusted.

God's *charis* is yours too! If you will only put your trust in God, he will pour his favor, his grace, his *charis*, his help, and his influence on you! But, despite all the wonderful blessings that spring from

God's *charis*, does receiving it mean you'll get everything you want for Christmas? Nope!

Mary had God's favor, his grace, his *charis*, his help and influence in her life—but she still had trouble. She had to travel on a donkey, stay with the animals, and then run for her life when Herod wanted to kill her baby.

If you think life is going to be easy just because you trust God, you are sadly mistaken. But the good news is that you don't need to be afraid, because God's influence and help are available to help you through your challenges.

GOOD NEWS IS FROM GOD

...the angel said to [the shepherds], "Do not be afraid; for behold, I bring you good news of great joy which will be for all the people..."
—Luke 2:10

The final "fear not" that we will look at is the one told to the shepherds.

Many people live with horrible fear, even at this festive time of year. They worry especially about money. They hurt from many wounds, some of which are self-inflicted. They also fear terribly about the future. If I was one of the shepherds, I would probably freak out too if an angel suddenly stood before me! They may have even been wondering "Is he here to kill us?"—but the reason the angel appeared was to give good news.

Decades later, this same good news was proclaimed in the Gospel of John:

. . . God so loved the world, that He gave His only begotten Son, that whoever believes in Him shall not perish, but have eternal life. For God did not send the Son into the world to judge the world, but that the world might be saved through Him.

—John 3:16-17

Isn't it interesting that the Great Shepherd was announced first to shepherds? King David wrote:

The Lord is my shepherd;
*   I have all that I need.*
He lets me rest in green meadows;
*   he leads me beside peaceful streams.*
*   He renews my strength.*
He guides me along right paths,
*   bringing honor to his name.*
Even when I walk
*   through the darkest valley,*
I will not be afraid,
*   for you are close beside me.*

—Psalm 23:1-4, NLT

That's pretty good news, isn't it?

Some nine-year-old children were once asked what they thought of death and dying. Jim said, "When you die, they bury you in the ground and your soul goes to heaven, but your body can't go to heaven because it's too crowded up there already." Judy said, "Only the good people go to heaven. The other people go where it's

18

hot all the time like in Florida." John said, "Maybe I'll die someday, but I hope I don't die on my birthday because it's no fun to celebrate your birthday if you're dead." Marsha commented, "When you die, you don't have to do homework in heaven, unless your teacher is there too."

We don't need to fear death or trouble, because the good news is that a Savior, Christ the Lord, was born. The good news inspired an angel choir to start singing, and it also gives us so much joy that we want to share the good news about Jesus with the world!

The phrase "fear of the Lord" is mentioned eighteen times in Proverbs. Fear is always bad—unless it's in God. God is all-powerful. God is totally in control. He has no rival. The wise person will fear God and not man, or even Satan. God is almighty and able to justly condemn, but he loves you. He truly loves you, so you need not fear trouble, your past, your present, or your future.

If I were to give my credit card and PIN to you I would have to totally trust you. You would have the ability to truly do me harm. Well, God knows everything about you and me: he knows the secret sins; he knows everything. He has your "credit card" and "PIN," but you can trust him today.

Agape is a Greek word found in the New Testament that we translate as "love." God *agapes* you! He doesn't just care for you—he loves you so much that he gave his Son so that you might have everlasting life. I've given you four "fear nots," but I want to give you a "fear." Fear God!

Don't be afraid of anything else. When we allow fear to be a part of our lives, we're saying that something is more powerful than God. Let your respect for God be so deep that you give yourself to him—not just now, but every day you are on this earth. We are not to be scared of our Father but to come to him with grateful hearts, because he truly does love us!

chapter three

CHRISTMAS WITH A SPECIAL RELATIVE

Rick and Judy Armstrong had a hectic holiday schedule. The couple knew that they would be short of time, so they had a printer print their signature on their Christmas cards, instead of signing each one. Soon they started getting cards from friends signed "The Modest Morrisons," "The Clever Clarks," and "The Successful Smiths." Then they discovered the stationer's subtle mistake. She had mailed out a hundred cards that read "Happy Holidays from the Rich Armstrongs."

To many of us, Christmas is a special time that we may spend with our relatives. Our thoughts are filled with memories of Christmases past that we enjoyed with the family. They were so warm and comfy.

Christmas can be difficult when it is not shared with our closest loved ones. There is one special relative that we desperately need to spend Christmas with—it's Jesus Christ. The Bible teaches that he is the closest relative to all of humanity. We can't truly experience Christmas without him.

In Genesis 3, we read that when sin entered the world, things dramatically changed. Pain, trouble and death became a reality. But another reality is that God did not give up on his creation.

He could have wiped everything and everyone away, and if he had, he would have been totally just.

Isaiah 53:6 says that "All we like sheep have gone astray" (KJV). Like Adam and Eve, we have told God—the creator of all that is—that we want to run our own lives and know better than him. God calls this sin, and sin has terrible consequences. But God said, as we previously saw in the first prophecy, that the offspring of Eve would triumph over the tempter (Genesis 3:15).

The Apostle Paul described the state that all of humanity was in, and how the triumph of God changed everything:

> *You were dead because of your sins and because your sinful nature was not yet cut away. Then God made you alive with Christ, for he forgave all our sins. He canceled the record of the charges against us and took it away by nailing it to the cross. In this way, he disarmed the spiritual rulers and authorities. He shamed them publicly by his victory over them on the cross.*

—Colossians 2:13-15, NLT

God was not willing that anyone should perish, but that we all would have everlasting life, so...

GOD SENT HIS SON

The significance of Jesus Christ's coming is history-making. No other birth has had such an impact on humanity. The world historian and writer H. G. Wells, when asked who has left the greatest historical legacy, replied "Jesus stands first."[3]

So why did God send his Son? Here are a few reasons given in the gospel of John:

- To do the Father's will (John 6:38)
- To bear witness to the truth (John 18:37)
- To bring light to the darkness (John 12:46)
- To bring true judgment (John 9:39)
- To bring abundant life (John 10:10)

When humanity turned its back on its creator, only one being could step in and mediate between God and man. It had to be someone who could give his life to redeem humanity, and it had to be someone who was perfect—a pure offering. That one was the second person of the trinity, who came and clothed himself in flesh. Jesus Christ is 100% God, and he is 100% man. In other words, he is humankind's closest relative. He has taken on the responsibility of redeeming all of humanity, who had enslaved themselves to sin.

---

3 N.B. Hardeman, 1943, *The Dallas Lectures for 1943*, Dallas: Eugene S. Smith, p. 122

Sometimes in ancient Israel, a poor person was forced to sell part of his property or himself into slavery. But his nearest of kin could step in and "buy back" what his relative was forced to sell (Leviticus 25:48). For this reason, besides the obvious ones, family was very, very important. We see this illustrated in the book of Ruth, in Jeremiah 32, and, in a wonderful way, in Revelation 5. The kinsman redeemer was a rich relative who freed the debtor by paying the ransom price.

Sin ravages a life. It can make a person poor—and not only financially. Sin works quietly, by making a person simply ignore God. The sinful heart feels no need. It leads a person to truly believe there isn't anything wrong with cheating, lying, hating, or not forgiving. Sin blinds!

Not speaking of the dangers of sin is like taking a bottle of poison and changing the label. The label may say "juice," but the bottle still contains poison. Sin destroys everything it touches; destruction is its very nature. Sin binds, it chokes, it steals, it distorts, it confuses. Sin effectively renders a person unable to live in obedience to God. When sin is finished with a person, it brings death (James 1:15). You and I were created for more than this.

The good news is that God sent his Son to be born and to be our nearest relative. He came to redeem us, to buy us back. Our redemption is precious. Salvation has been purchased at a great and personal cost, because the Lord Jesus gave Himself for our sins in order to deliver us from them. Our forgiveness is based on the ransom price of the shed blood of Jesus Christ.

Incidentally, don't get hung up on the term "Son of God." God is Spirit and does not have physical offspring. The term is used to show the relationship between the first person (Father) of the deity and the second (Son). My son, Jeremy, is not the son of my flesh. Carole and I adopted him when he was ten months old. Sonship is about relationship. In fact, Adam was called "son of God" in the genealogy of Luke 3. In addition, the apostle Paul wrote, *"you are all sons of God through faith in Christ Jesus"* (Galatians 3:26). The second person of the Godhead has always existed, but entered the world in human form when he was born to his mother, Mary, in a small town called Bethlehem.

On one occasion, a cookbook was recalled by the manufacturer. Now, I don't know about you, but I've never heard of a cookbook being recalled before. I've heard of cars, toasters and baby seats being recalled, but never a cookbook.

It turns out that this cookbook had been recalled because one recipe had left out an important ingredient. And the producers of the book realized that if someone followed the directions of that recipe and left out that ingredient, the ingredients they put together could actually blow up in their faces. So because of that hazard, the cookbook was recalled.

I thought to myself, "There must be a sermon there somewhere." You see, God has given us the recipe for life. He says, "You want peace? Then here is the recipe. Find forgiveness through Jesus Christ. Live according to my principles, the ingredients that make it all possible." But if you leave out some of his ingredients, or include some of the ingredients of the world, then what happens? Life can blow up in your face. That's why there is so much depression, so much suicide, and so much rejection today. Too many are following the wrong recipes for life.

"In [Jesus] we have redemption through His blood, the forgiveness of our trespasses, according to the riches of His grace which He lavished on us" (Ephesians 1:7-8). The redemptive work of Jesus Christ delivers anyone who believes in him from their slavery to sin. Salvation is not based on the merits of what we do, but solely on the coming of the Son of God, his death and resurrection.

> *. . .the grace of God has appeared, bringing salvation to all men, instructing us to deny ungodliness and worldly desires and to live sensibly, righteously and godly in the present age, looking for the blessed hope and the appearing of the glory of our great God and Savior, Christ Jesus, who gave Himself for us to redeem us from every lawless deed, and to purify for Himself a people for His own possession, zealous for good deeds.*
>
> —Titus 2:11-14

GOD DOES NOT CONDEMN THOSE WHO ARE IN CHRIST

The Bible reminds us that *"all have sinned"* (Romans 3:23). God could easily have judged us as unworthy of redemption, but he didn't. We already have seen that God would have been just in condemning the world, but he didn't, so why would anyone worry that they are condemned? The only reason for condemnation is that a person is not "in Christ." Paul often wrote about a person's relationship with Jesus Christ. To be "in Christ" is to be in relationship with him. Many fingers are pointed at you, but they cannot condemn you if you have a relationship with Jesus Christ; neither can your past condemn you.

The apostle Paul reminded the Corinthians that *"if anyone is in Christ, he is a new creature; the old things passed away; behold, new things have come. Now all these things are from God, who reconciled us to Himself through Christ..."* (2 Corinthians 5:17-18).

Sin sticks like glue until we repent (confess our sin and choose to go God's way) and believe; then, the precious blood of Jesus cleanses us from all unrighteousness. So anyone who repents and believes is in right relationship with God. Relationship with God is not like a coat that you can take off and choose whether or not to wear depending on your daily mood. It's respecting the Creator and passionately desiring to know him more than anything else.

The apostle Paul was a murderer and persecutor of Christians, but after he repented and believed who Jesus is, he wrote:

> ...*whatever things were gain to me, those things I have counted as loss for the sake of Christ. More than that, I count all things to be loss in view of the surpassing value of knowing Christ Jesus my Lord, for whom I have suffered the loss of all things, and count them but rubbish so that I may gain Christ, and may be found in Him, not having a righteousness of my own derived from the Law, but that which is through faith in Christ, the righteousness which comes from God on the basis of faith.*

—Philippians 3:7-9

Paul also said that *"...the law of the Spirit of life in Christ Jesus has set you free from the law of sin and of death"* (Romans 8:2).

There are terrible consequences to sin—just ask Adam and Eve—but praise God that there is no condemnation for those who are in Christ. If you are in Christ, your standing hasn't merely improved; it has been completely changed! You don't simply have less condemnation in your life. You have *no* condemnation if you are in relationship with Jesus Christ.

You may be living apart from your parents or siblings. Some of your relatives may have passed away. Christmas might be sad for you because loneliness is knocking at the door of your heart. But I want you to know that your nearest relative is present. You are not alone if Jesus Christ is a part of your life. He came for you! Rest in that wonderful relationship.

> *Oh give thanks to the Lord, for He is good,*
> *For His lovingkindness is everlasting.*
> *Let the redeemed of the Lord say so,*
> *Whom He has redeemed from the hand of the adversary. . .*
> —Psalm 107:1-2

If you know Jesus Christ as your savior, rejoice! Celebrate his coming, no matter how difficult things have been. If you don't know Jesus Christ as your savior, I have good news! He loves you and came to this earth not to condemn you but to give you everlasting life.

Paul the Apostle said, *". . .Christ Jesus came into the world to save sinners. . ."* (I Timothy 1:15). In fact, Jesus himself said, *". . .God did not send the Son into the world to judge the world, but that the world might be saved through Him"* (John 3:17).

What is the Christmas story all about? You might think that the explanation is found in one of the gospel narratives. The truth is that the best explanation of the meaning of Christmas was written by the Apostle Paul.

> ...when the right time came, God sent his Son, born of a woman, subject to the law. God sent him to buy freedom for us who were slaves to the law, so that he could adopt us as his very own children.
>
> —Galatians 4:4-5, NLT

Our response to our nearest relative should be to surrender our lives to him. We do this not by following the old selfish ways we knew before we met Jesus, but by walking in the Spirit now and all year round.

chapter four

DANGEROUS CHRISTMAS

Christmas can be hazardous in various ways. Celebrating Christmas in countries where it's illegal to be a Christian can be perilous. In North America, a more common risk might be an electrical fire relating to a Christmas tree. One terrible Christmas, I was called to the Children's Hospital in Kansas City, Missouri. A Christmas tree electrical fire had resulted in the death of Angie and her three boys. It was horrific to see the bodies. Although decorations and presents were in place in their home, danger also lurked.

The first Christmas was also a treacherous time.

> ...*behold, an angel of the Lord appeared to Joseph in a dream and said, "Get up! Take the Child and His mother and flee to Egypt, and remain there until I tell you; for Herod is going to search for the Child to destroy Him."*
>
> *So Joseph got up and took the Child and His mother while it was still night, and left for Egypt. He remained there until the death of Herod.*

—Matthew 2:13-15

NO CHILD LIKE THIS CHILD

- Babies are fragile and in need of total care. Imagine being afraid of a baby! But there was something very unique about this one. Baby Jesus was a target because he was a threat not only to Herod, but to evil spiritual forces.

- Incredibly, God humbled himself and identified with us as a baby. He came with healing for a world that had become very dangerous. A baby—God came as a baby! To protect this helpless child, both the Magi and Joseph were warned about Herod, who felt threatened by his coming!

- Of course, Satan was threatened by this baby on an even deeper level, so you can be sure that he was whispering in Herod's ear. Oh, but this was not a baby like any other! Isaiah prophesied, as quoted by Matthew, "'BEHOLD, THE VIRGIN SHALL BE WITH CHILD AND SHALL BEAR A SON, AND THEY SHALL CALL HIS NAME IMMANUEL,' which translated means, 'GOD WITH US.'" (Matthew 1:23).

- The Son of God had over 100 titles and names including Immanuel, "God with us." God is so big and beyond our understanding that he is always present—but in a baby, God came to be with us!

Tens of thousands of people make their homes at a dump site in Manila, Philippines. It's a dangerous place. Some people have been born, grown up, and died there without ever going anywhere else, even in the city of Manila. It is an amazing thing. But there are missionaries, including my brother-in-law, who have chosen to leave their own country and its comforts to show the love of Jesus Christ to these people by living with them in a garbage dump. Amazing, yes—but not as amazing as the journey from heaven to earth. The creator came to be with us in a dangerous dump site called Earth! Some may ask, "Why does humanity need God with us?" The answer was given to Isaiah the prophet.

> *Behold, the Lord's hand is not so short*
> *That it cannot save;*
> *Nor is His ear so dull*
> *That it cannot hear.*
> *But your iniquities have made a separation between you and your*
> *God, And your sins have hidden His face from you so that He does*
> *not hear.*

—Isaiah 59:1-2)

These words were spoken originally to the covenant people of Israel, but the principle applies to all who have sinned against the Creator, which includes you and me. *"If we say that we have no sin, we are deceiving ourselves and the truth is not in us"* (1 John 1:8). *"The Lord has looked down from heaven upon the sons of men, to see if there are any who understand, who seek after God. They have all turned aside; together they have become corrupt; there is no one who does good, not even one"* (Psalm 14:2-3). *"For whoever keeps the whole law and yet stumbles in one point, he has become guilty of all"* (James 2:10).

I was separated from my Creator and on my way to destruction because of my sin, and so were you. Humankind seeks to find a replacement to make the gnawing emptiness go away. Why do people who do not accept Christ as their Savior still put up Christmas lights, buy gifts, and celebrate? Could it be that they sense a deep void (even if they don't admit to it), a deep emptiness that they try to fill—possibly without even knowing it. The loneliness (especially at this time of year) can be overwhelming—and worse, it is dangerous. But God reaches out to us in those times of loneliness, and will even set things in motion for us to encounter him.

Sadly, there are many people who have allowed their sin to separate them from other people, as well as from the God who desires to be close to them.

Baby Jesus was like no other baby. He was dangerous to this selfish, sinful world. Herod was threatened by him—and more than thirty years later, others were plotting to kill him, again because there was no one like him.

Peter Hitchens, the brother of the famous atheist Christopher Hitchens, once had a need in his heart to hear some Christmas carols, so he went into a church just to listen to the singing. God is sneaky! Peter Hitchens heard the truth in song and gave his life to Jesus Christ. God drew close! Everyone is on his radar, including the atheist!

The writer to the Hebrews put it this way: *"Because God's children are human beings—made of flesh and blood—the Son also became flesh and blood. For only as a human being could he die, and only by dying could he break the power of the devil, who had the power of death"* (Hebrews 2:14, NLT). He also wrote, *"We do not have a high priest who cannot sympathize with our weaknesses, but One who has been tempted in all things as we are, yet without sin. Therefore let us draw near with confidence to the throne of grace, so that we may receive mercy and find grace to help in time of need"* (Hebrews 4:15-16).

Jesus Christ understands us. He came! More people become depressed at this time of year than any other. Christmas can be a dangerous time, with suicide happening and darkness dwelling within just a few feet of bright lights and laughter—but the greatest danger of Christmas would be to miss just who the child born in Bethlehem is. Either we bow and worship like the shepherds and magi (wise men) did, or we will bow in fear when confronted by a holy God on the day of judgment.

Jesus Christ came as a baby to a dangerous world because he loves this world. He did not come to condemn the world, but to save it.

chapter five

DRIFTING THROUGH CHRISTMAS

A wise pastor once wrote, "Everybody today is asking, in the face of some of the tragic things that are happening, 'What's wrong with humanity? What's wrong with life? Why is the world in a continual mess? Why all this murder and violence and evil?' The answer of Scripture universally is, 'Man's sin.'" [4]

The stark contrast between the sin and evil we see every day, and the joyousness that people are told they should have at Christmastime, can be quite puzzling. Loneliness and pain are felt more in December than any other time of the year. How can anyone have a happy holiday when suffering seems to surround us?

Listen to the angels, who were very much a part of that first Christmas. Angels spoke to Mary and to a group of shepherds, and their message was good news. One angel said, *"I bring you good news of great joy which will be for all the people; for today in the city of David there has been born for you a Savior, who is Christ the Lord"* (Luke 2:10-11).

---

4   http://www.raystedman.org/daily-devotions/hebrews/the-power-to-cleanse

A Savior

Romans 3 reminds us that the whole world is guilty and in need of this Savior. It's hard to see ourselves as no better than the worst sinner, but the truth is that a Savior was born for all people—including you and me! That's good news!

But because we run the risk of missing what Christmas is really all about, Christmas can be a dangerous season.

People usually take one of three approaches to Christmas:

- Commercialism/Secularism, which leads to a false Christmas based on selfishness and appeals to the flesh. It is selfish and temporal, but it's very popular.
- False Religiosity, which also appeals to the "me." In this approach, God becomes a heavenly Santa Claus who does things for our comforts. Followers of this approach might be characterized by hedonism and narcissism that are masked by piously praying for what is desired. This false religiosity appeases our guilty conscience when we do something for someone else.
- The Master Plan, which metaphorically keeps the cross near the manger. In this approach, we always remember that Jesus came to be the sacrifice to pay for our sins.

The first two approaches may sound appealing, but actually they miss the true meaning of Christmas. For instance, some say

Drifting Through Christmas

Christmas is about family and friends, but what happens in cases of loss or estrangement from loved ones? Christmas becomes a difficult and sad time instead of celebrating the good news that a Savior came for all people. Others say that Christmas is for giving to those who are less fortunate, but that again takes the focus away from the good news of a Savior. Giving to others is something that should take place all year round—but to make it the centerpiece of Christmas tempts us to forget that no amount of kindness will cleanse us of our sin and our need of a Savior. The good news of great joy is that a Savior was born, which indicates that all people were sinners destined for judgment.

Our challenge now is to resist drifting away from the good news of that first Christmas.

The story is told of a farmer who died and had willed his farm to the Devil. In the court, they didn't quite know what to do with it—how do you give a farm to the Devil? The judge decided: "The best way to carry out the wishes of the deceased is to allow the farm to grow weeds, the soil to erode, and the house and barn to rot. In our opinion, the best way to leave something to the Devil is to do nothing." We can leave our lives to the Devil the same way: doing nothing, drifting with whatever currents will drive us.

> *...we must pay much closer attention to what we have heard, so that we do not drift away from it. For if the word spoken through angels proved unalterable, and every transgression and disobedience received a just penalty, how will we escape if we neglect so great a salvation?*
> —Hebrews 2:1-3

Even though the lights, Santa Claus, presents, and food can distract us from what Christmas is truly about, we must pay close attention to what the angels said. They brought the wonderful gospel message of the Savior's birth. Drifting away from Jesus as the central focus of Christmas, and the answer to man's sin, can be very subtle.

Ever since the Garden of Eden, humanity has tried all kinds of ways to fix the problem of sin. But we can't. It's impossible! There's nothing wrong with information, technology, money, and pleasure. They're just the wrong tools to fix the problem. It's like trying to fix a tractor with a circular saw. As we discussed earlier, we are saved only *"by grace. . .through faith"* (Ephesians 2:8). Grace means that it is by God's doing that we are saved. It's always been that way.

Abraham was saved that way and so were all the Old Testament saints before the coming of the Savior; now we are saved solely by the work of God. That is the good news!

Some are tempted by creature comforts and a focus on quick, temporary pleasures—but the angels brought the message that a Savior had been born! Jesus came because you and I were hopelessly caught in sin. Christmas is about a Savior!

Satan can tempt us to trust in secularism or false religiosity—things that will superficially make us feel good—and there are plenty of teachers and preachers out there that will tickle the ear and dangle shiny pleasures in front of us. But we are talking about the reality and truth of Christmas. Any other message will result in drifting from the truth.

CHRIST THE LORD

Imagine! The baby in the manger was the Lord, the Master. God the Son humbled himself to be dependent on Mary's care. The good news was more than that a Savior had been born, but also that this baby was Lord. We read that the Lord is our shepherd (Psalm 23); the disciples were taught to pray with the Lord's Prayer, and we know that there is a day coming called "the Day of the Lord."

The apostle Paul exults about the Lord in the first chapter of Ephesians. Jesus Christ is truly Lord. It's his way and no other.

Some might ask, "Then isn't Jesus no better than a tyrant?" This question ignores that he came as a baby, with humility and love for all. For true life, we must take his way and no other! We may be tempted to accept Jesus as Savior but to make ourselves Lord. Not possible! The baby born in the stable is Savior *and* Lord. He's a package deal!

It's our choice as to whether we will receive the good news or not. In his great sermon, Jesus asked, "Why do you call me 'Lord, Lord,' and do not do what I say?" (Luke 6:46). In the same sermon he said,

> *Not everyone who says to Me, "Lord, Lord" will enter the kingdom of heaven, but he who does the will of My Father who is in heaven will enter. Many will say to Me on that day, "Lord, Lord, did we not prophesy in Your name, and in Your name cast out demons, and in Your name perform many miracles?" And then I will declare to them "I never knew you; depart from me, you who practice lawlessness"*
>
> —Matthew 7:21-23

Some have religion but do not know the Savior, the Lord who was laid in a manger. The context of what Jesus was saying is obvious. A person acknowledges Jesus Christ as Lord when they live in obedience to his will. He makes his will plain in Matthew 5-7. Showing love through forgiveness, humility, and service reveals that Jesus is Lord. Have you ever heard the Holy Spirit tell you to witness to or forgive someone, and your former self says "No"? Our fleshly selves do not like the Lordship of Jesus Christ, but we are to put to death daily the way we used to live before meeting him.

The Apostle Paul said, *"I have been crucified with Christ; and it is no longer I who live, but Christ lives in me; and the life which I now live in the flesh I live by faith in the Son of God, who loved me and gave Himself up for me"* (Galatians 2:20).

- Pastor Tim Dilena said, "Real Christianity is a demonstration, not a declaration."[5]
- The world says, "You say you're a Christian; show me!"
- Jesus Christ the Lord said, *"This is My commandment, that you love one another. . ."* (John 15:12)

Notice that Jesus the Lord does not ask us to do something that he does not do himself. No one has ever loved like he did! The good news for all people is that Jesus Christ, not an evil tyrant, is Lord. His ways are not destructive, but restorative and life-giving.

---

5   In a sermon preached in Brooklyn, New York, 2013.

The angels had a message that humankind needed to hear. It was the good news of great joy that a Savior, Christ the Lord, had been born. But the winds of commercialism and religiosity blow very strong, and many drift from the truth of the gospel. The author of Hebrews wrote, "Pay attention!" (chapter 2). You may think that you're not distracted, or in the least tempted to miss the true meaning of Christmas—but in 1989 Americans used 28,497,464 rolls and sheets of wrapping paper; 16,826,362 packages of tags and bows; 372,430,684 greeting cards; and 35,200,000 Christmas trees during the holiday season.

There's no reason to believe the consumption rate is any less now.

Satan's plan is to distract and to offer counterfeits to the truth, but the wise will keep their eyes on Jesus Christ, our Lord and Savior. Nothing can compare with him.

The amazing declaration of Scripture is that the reason the Creator of the world became the Babe of Bethlehem was to wash away people's unwashable stains. The good news of Christmas, of course, is that every one of us who has found Christ, who has come to him, and who follows him finds again and again that he has the power to cleanse us. Jesus has the power to put away the guilt of the past, whether the patterns of the past fifty years of life or the past five minutes. He has the power to cleanse it and wash it away, and to set us on our feet again.

It's our choice. Either drift away from the truth that Jesus Christ is Savior and Lord, or focus on him and join with the angels, the shepherds, and the magi in worshiping him.

chapter six

GOD'S CHRISTMAS GIFT

I f someone sends us a Christmas gift and we aren't home, a card is left in the mail box announcing that we can retrieve the parcel by coming to the post office. The announcement of God's gift came in a way that most of us would not have dreamt. In fulfillment of prophecy, God's Christmas Gift had no fanfare in typical earthly ways, but God does things in amazing ways.

Instead of Caesar, shepherds were told that the Savior had finally arrived.

Most Jews were looking for a political Savior to free them from the brutal Romans, but God had a gift for all of humanity.

This is an important fact that we should all remember. God's Christmas gift is sent not just to make us feel better in this life, but to change our lives. Few gifts we give or receive change a life, but God's Christmas gift does. Jesus Christ has changed lives. He turned a murderer into a minister (Saul of Tarsus into Paul the apostle). Aren't you glad that Jesus changed your life? If you need a change in your life, read the rest very carefully.

Luke wrote,

. . .there was a man in Jerusalem named Simeon. He was righteous and devout and was eagerly waiting for the Messiah to come and rescue Israel. The Holy Spirit was upon him and had revealed to him that he would not die until he had seen the Lord's Messiah. That day the Spirit led him to the Temple. So when Mary and Joseph came to present the baby Jesus to the Lord as the law required, Simeon was there. He took the child in his arms and praised God, saying,

"Sovereign Lord, now let your servant die in peace, as you have promised. I have seen your salvation, which you have prepared for all people. He is a light to reveal God to the nations, and he is the glory of your people Israel!"

—Luke 2:25-32, NLT

God's Christmas gift is...

A LIGHT OF REVELATION TO THE NATIONS

The world lies in darkness. The world has no real insight as to how to address the multitude of problems it faces. Some suggest more education, but we already have many books on every topic and we have the same horrible problems that seemingly have no end. Others suggest that communication is the key to change, but we have multiple ways to communicate with others and yet darkness, misunderstanding, and trouble hover over humanity. Pick up any newspaper and you will immediately see the headlines: the greenhouse effect, AIDS, drugs, toxic waste, moral decay, and terrorism. The result is that people are fearful and angry. They live isolated lives. They don't have much hope for the future. They are living in a dark, cold place, but Jesus Christ is a light of revelation to a world in darkness caused by sin.

Some don't see a problem in their sin, because sin and the enemy of their souls have darkened their spiritual sight. However, God's Christmas Gift is a light of revelation to all people. James wrote, "Humble yourselves in the presence of the Lord" (James 4:10). God calls us to put aside our lifelong crusade to defend ourselves, promote ourselves, preserve our possessions, protect our reputations, and prolong our lives.

God is our provider, our defender, our hope, and our destiny. The false illusion that we can get our own lives together must be exposed to the light, to Jesus, *"the Light of the world"* (John 8:12).

> *. . .if we walk in the light, as [God] Himself is in the Light, we have fellowship with one another, and the blood of Jesus His Son cleanses us from all sin.*
>
> —I John 1:7

Isaiah the prophet wrote regarding the Messiah to the nation of Israel:

> *Arise, shine; for your light has come,*
> *And the glory of the Lord has risen upon you.*
> *For behold, darkness will cover the earth*
> *And deep darkness the peoples;*
> *But the Lord will rise upon you*
> *And His glory will appear upon you.*

Nations will come to your light.
And kings to the brightness of your rising.

—Isaiah 60:1-3

Jesus said, *"I am the Light of the world; he who follows Me will not walk in the darkness, but will have the Light of life"* (John 8:12). In his prayer, Simeon prophesied that Jesus would bring light to those in darkness. When anyone encounters the light of the world, they are faced with the glory of God and their sin is exposed.

Like Adam and Eve, humankind tries to hide from God. It's sad but true. The good news is that Jesus Christ is the light. Walking in darkness is dangerous—try walking in your home at night with no light. The metaphor of Jesus as the light is seen throughout scripture and is very important for us to catch because light is extremely delicate, subtle, pure, brilliant and powerful. Darkness cannot stay when light comes.

When the sun peeks through the clouds, we enjoy the warmth and light, but it also shows the dust and dirt that was hidden in the dark. When the angel appeared to the shepherds, the glory (*doxa* in the Greek) shone around them. This word literally means the brilliance and splendor of who God is.

The angel said, *"Do not be afraid"* (Luke 2:10). Often when encountering the truth of who God is, humans will become fearful because their sinfulness is exposed. But God does not condemn: he is the light that has come to show how much we need him. Confession and repentance are wonderful things. In fact, *". . .the kindness of God leads you to repentance"* (Romans 2:4). God is not willing that anyone should perish, and hopes that all will repent (2 Peter 3:9).

Repentance simply means to say we are wrong and God is right, and then go God's way. It's a good thing to be called to repentance.

The Psalmist David wrote, *"The Lord is my light and my salvation; whom shall I fear? The Lord is the defense of my life; whom shall I dread?"* (Psalm 27:1). As the darkness races away when the sun rises, so ignorance and error flee away when Jesus gives light to the mind. We respond to who God is by repenting and living in the light of relationship with him.

God's Christmas gift is...

THE GLORY OF GOD'S PEOPLE ISRAEL

The Jewish people have been the most oppressed people throughout history. They have been hated and persecuted—millions died in the Nazi holocaust, but they survive, despite their persecutions.

The majority are in trapped in unbelief, with only a few believing that Jesus is the Messiah. Israel's survival is evidence of God's promised care and continued plan for them, according to His covenant.

God has not given up on Israel, but why is that significant for you and me?

There is a dangerous teaching that says all of the promises of God to Israel have been transferred to the Church. This is not logical or biblical. God is not willing that anyone perish, neither Jew nor Gentile.

The word Israel is used 73 times in the New Testament, but not once is it used for the Church. And God treats Israel differently than the Church. In Romans, Paul wrote of his countrymen: *"They are the people of Israel, chosen to be God's adopted children. God revealed his glory to them. He made covenants with them and gave them his law. He gave them the privilege of worshiping him and receiving his wonderful promises"* (Romans 9:4, NLT). On top of that, Jesus was born to Mary, a Jew.

He was, and is, the brightness or glory of his people, Israel. Jesus, from the moment of his birth, has been a Jew. This is an incredible truth. God chose the descendants of Abraham and Sarah, who became the nation of Israel, to be His people. They were charged to walk by faith and show God's glory. God made a covenant with Abraham (Genesis 17) and his descendants, but Israel failed to walk by faith and show the glory of God to the rest of the world.

After 430 years of Israel's disobedience, God gave what some call the "law" to Moses. We have made a mistake in translating the Jewish word *Torah* to the English word "law." What God gave Moses was teaching, a path to walk in for life. It did not replace or invalidate the covenant of faith made with Abraham; rather, it was given to reveal sinfulness and prepare the nation for their promised Messiah (Galatians 3:16-19, 23-24; Romans 7:9-13).

Through the teaching given to Moses, we have the knowledge of sin. For example, a traffic sign shows visually if the law is being broken, but that sign forces no one to obey. When the Son of God, the Messiah, came to Israel, the nation as a whole rejected him. One cannot become a child of God through genealogy (God has no grandchildren); this can take place only through faith in the Messiah, the promised seed of Abraham:

> *. . .it is not as though the word of God has failed. For they are not all Israel who are descended from Israel; nor are they all children*

because they are Abraham's descendants, but: "through Isaac your descendants will be named." That is, it is not the children of the flesh who are children of God, but the children of the promise are regarded as descendants.

—Romans 9:6-8

The Church did not replace Israel; it is both a fulfillment and a continuation of the Abrahamic covenant. The love of God for His creation was expressed when His Son, the Lord Jesus Christ, gave himself up for us. The angel said to the shepherds that he was bringing *"good news of great joy which will be for all the people"* (Luke 2:10). This included both Jew and Gentile.

Who doesn't need some good news? If you're an optimist you're looking for good news. If you're a pessimist you're expecting bad news. A farmer went to his banker and announced that he had bad news and good news. He said, "First the bad news...I can't make my mortgage payments. I can't pay off the crop loan that I've taken out for 10 years, and I won't be able to pay you the couple hundred thousand I still have outstanding on my tractors and other equipment." The banker asked, "What's the good news?" The farmer replied, "The good news is that I'm going to keep banking with you!" We're like the farmer; we have had it bad because we've sinned—but the good news is that God hasn't given up on anyone.

God the Creator, who is love, who is kind, who is patient, who is all-powerful, and who is holy, gave the best Christmas gift that you or I will ever receive. Unlike the presents we get, his Christmas gift is one that will never grow old or useless.

Think back to five years ago. Can you remember what you received from people for Christmas?

Let's make it easier. How about one year ago. Can you remember what you received for Christmas?

If you have received the forgiveness of sins and have a relationship with Jesus Christ through faith, you have the greatest Christmas gift.

If you have not placed your faith Jesus Christ yet, today is your day. God has the greatest Christmas gift waiting for you. Receive God's Christmas gift, Jesus Christ. Repent—it's a good thing—and accept him as your Lord and Savior today by surrendering your life to him, as millions have already done.

chapter seven

PLACED UNDER THE TREE

A Christmas tradition that many observe is placing presents under a decorated evergreen tree. Under another tree, a Gift was placed for sinners, but the sad fact is that most will never receive this gift. They simply leave it under the tree.

During his crucifixion, Jesus prayed, *"'Father forgive them; for they do not know what they are doing.' And they cast lots, dividing up His garments among themselves"* (Luke 23:34). When the blood of Jesus pooled at the foot of the cross, God's amazing gift of forgiveness was left for everyone to unwrap! Jesus gave his lifeblood—and oh, how wonderful is the truth that he gave humanity his forgiveness.

As wonderful as it is for you and me to forgive each other, it can't compare to the forgiveness of God, because when we sin against each other, we are sinning against other sinners. Choosing whether or not to extend forgiveness to each other is not an option for us. We must forgive people who hurt us, since we too hurt others. Conversely, God is holy and worthy of our love and total worship. He has done something remarkable. He has forgiven us!

FORGIVENESS WAS GIVEN

The apostle John wrote, *"If we confess our sins, he is faithful and righteous to forgive us our sins and to cleanse us from all unrighteousness"* (1 John 1:9). And the Psalmist wrote, *". . .you offer forgiveness, that we might learn to fear you"* (Psalm 130:4, NLT).

Some don't believe they have anything to be forgiven. "It's only wrong if I call it wrong." "Nobody can impose a morality on me." Have you heard anything like this? Still, it's hard to recall what Hitler did or what a rapist did and deny it was wrong. Something deep down inside us tells us that lying or stealing is wrong. No one has to tell you what is wrong and right. God has already written it on the hearts of all humankind. But God has done more! He has offered forgiveness.

I have heard some ask, "Why doesn't God just forgive sin?" When we sin—and all of us have—there is a penalty since sin actually denies who God is. For instance, stealing denies God's ability to provide everything we need. Try to recall a time when someone treated you badly—a righteous anger for justice boiled in you. There was a demand for the wrong to be made right. You and I can go to God and say "we are sorry" for sinning, but we need the gift of God's forgiveness!

Have you ever said you're sorry only to have the other person say "That's all right," but you can sense that they really haven't forgiven you and are going to hold it against you anyway? No matter how sincere a mass murderer is when he says he is sorry and won't do it again, justice will not allow what was done to be wiped away.

The law doesn't care that you're sorry! God's forgiveness is desperately needed.

So to leave God's gift under the tree without taking it is not only sad, it's deadly!

Jesus asked the Father to forgive sinners, and the Father forgave them on the basis of the blood that was shed on the cross. Jesus paid the debt of every sinner, but there are still two choices for everyone—thankfully receive the gift of forgiveness, or despise God by resisting the gift and rebelling.

Prayers for the Blind were Given

Notice that after Jesus was crucified, people were playing games. Just like children will sit under the Christmas tree with toys that they just unwrapped, soldiers were playing games at the foot of the cross. They didn't see what was happening. They were blind to their need of forgiveness, but God wasn't! Humanity was dead, oblivious to their need. The prophet Isaiah wrote, hundreds of years before Jesus Christ hung on the cross, that he would pray for sinners (Isaiah 53:12), and sure enough, he did.

The work of the Holy Spirit is to bring us to the place of understanding so we can see just what sin has done. What did Jesus mean when he said, "They don't know what they are doing"? The soldiers were professionals at execution. They knew how to torture a man, but they were blind to their sin.

The apostle John wrote, *"If we say that we have no sin, we are deceiving ourselves and the truth is not in us"* (1 John 1:8). Sin has an insidious way of blinding us to our need. It deceives! Jesus prayed that humankind would really see just what we are doing when we sin, so that we would repent and receive the gift of God's forgiveness.

Sadly, many ignore the work of the Holy Spirit and continue to refuse forgiveness. In fact, Jesus said that one day people will say "Lord, Lord" and he will say, "I never knew you" (Matthew 7:22-23).

One of the greatest tragedies for people would be to live in darkness when they could live in the light.

Rose Crawford had been blind for 50 years. Then she had an operation in an Ontario hospital. She said, "I just can't believe it," as the doctor lifted the bandages from her eyes. She wept when, for the first time in her life, a dazzling and beautiful world of form and color greeted her eyes She could now see. The amazing thing about her story, however, was that 20 years of her blindness were unnecessary. She didn't know that surgical techniques had been developed two decades earlier that could have cured her, and she had continued in her blindness for many years.

Jesus forgave people! *"[People] brought to Him a paralytic lying on a bed. Seeing their faith, Jesus said to the paralytic, 'Take courage, son; your sins are forgiven'"* (Matthew 9:2). Speaking to a known sinner who repented, Jesus said, *"Your sins have been forgiven"* (Luke 7:48).

Jesus was on the cross in our place, as our representative. It was well within his power to have called ten thousand or more angels to his rescue. He could have let loose thunderbolts of wrath against those who crucified him. He could have caused the earth to open its mouth so that his torturers would go down alive into the pit of hell. It was well within his power to do all of this, but then his suffering would no longer have been as one of us, in our place, and as our representative.

When he represented us upon the cross, Jesus was no longer in a place of authority and power. He was there as one with us, one of us, and one for us—totally dependent upon the grace and mercy of God. So he prayed, *"Father, forgive them, for they do not know what they are doing"* (Luke 23:34).

What is the greatest gift we have ever received? What is the greatest gift we can give anyone?

I want to remind you that there is a wonderful gift that remains under the tree, waiting to be unpacked and enjoyed! It is the forgiveness of God. Should you minimize this gift, these words of Jesus will help to show just what a great gift has been given to you and me:

Pray, then, in this way:
"Our Father who is in heaven,
Hallowed be Your name.
Your kingdom come.
Your will be done,
On earth as it is in heaven.
Give us this day our daily bread.
And forgive us our debts, as we also have forgiven our debtors.
And do not lead us into temptation, but deliver us from evil. For Yours
is the kingdom and the power and the glory forever. Amen."

—Matthew 6:9-13

Everyone needs to call upon the forgiveness of God, especially the author of this book. Forgiveness is required for those who have been forgiven, because God forgives. If you or I are unforgiving in our hearts, then we are living in contradiction to who God is—and that is sinful. Jesus came to this world that we might have life, and that more abundantly. The forgiveness he gives makes this possible, and our forgiving others makes it happen!

chapter eight

THE GLORY OF GOD

When the angels came to tell the shepherds of Jesus' birth, the angel choir sang, *"Glory to God in the highest, and on earth peace among men with whom He is pleased"* (Luke 2:14). Let's meditate on this powerful statement. Peace can be maintained by force in any society, but only God can bring peace in our lives. That special, deep-down peace comes when everything is as God created it to be. God's glory does fill the earth, but sin has messed things up.

In fact, the Apostle Paul wrote, *". . .all have sinned and come short of the glory of God"* (Romans 3:23).

I used to read this verse and think that it meant that I had not measured up to who God is, something which seems impossible—but let's look at something else Paul wrote: *"By him all things were created, both in the heavens and on earth, visible and invisible, whether thrones or dominions or rulers. . .through Him and for Him"* (Colossians 1:16).

You were created for God's glory, to show how wonderful he is, and to represent his greatness. So sin wrecks what you were made for. Some may be tempted to think "that means God doesn't want me to have desires." Wrong! Jesus said, *"Whatever you ask in My name, that will I do, so that the Father may be glorified in the Son. If you ask Me anything in My name, I will do it"* (John 14:13-14). We continue to have desires, but they are filtered through the desire for the glory of God to be seen in us. Jesus doesn't tell us to ask for riches or an easy life. The purpose of our lives is to bring glory to God. That is why sin is so terrible: because it makes us less than what we were meant to be.

Our desire should be for the glory of God to be seen in our lives, instead of seeking what we think is important. Worrying, for example, won't be glory-filled. Peter wrote, *"Cast all your anxiety on him because he [Jesus Christ] cares for you"* (1 Peter 5:7, NIV). In other words, you really don't have a care when your life's motto is to live "For the Glory of God."

Our decisions, our attitudes, our ministries, our families, our homes, everything that makes us who we are, and all that we have are for the glory of the Lord! "God is most glorified in you when you are most satisfied in him,"[6] writes pastor and author John Piper.

> *The heavens proclaim the glory of God.*
> *The skies display his craftsmanship.*
> *Day after day they continue to speak;*
> *night after night they make him known.*
> *They speak without a sound or word;*
> *their voice is never heard.*

---

6   http://www.desiringgod.org/messages/god-is-most-glorified-in-us-when-we-are-most-satisfied-in-him

Yet their message has gone throughout the earth,
and their words to all the world.
God has made a home in the heavens for the sun.
It bursts forth like a radiant bridegroom after his wedding.
It rejoices like a great athlete eager to run the race.
The sun rises at one end of the heavens
and follows its course to the other end.
Nothing can hide from its heat.
The instructions of the Lord are perfect,
reviving the soul.
The decrees of the Lord are trustworthy,
making wise the simple.
The commandments of the Lord are right,
bringing joy to the heart.
The commands of the Lord are clear,
giving insight for living.

—Psalm 19:1-8, NLT

God is not a terrible, angry deity whom we have to appease. We know who God is by seeing Jesus Christ. God lovingly created all that is, and besides that, *". . .He rescued us from the domain of darkness, and transferred us to the kingdom of His beloved Son, in whom we have redemption, the forgiveness of sins"* (Colossians 1:13-14).

The Psalmist tells us that we glorify God by living our lives for him, and this happens as we pay attention to what he tells us. Consider a car or truck. When you buy it there are instructions, an owner's manual, that we must pay attention to for the vehicle to run properly. Gas, oil, tire pressure, and lights all must be attended to for the car or truck to run as it was designed. God also has instructions for our lives so that we will exist as we were created to be.

GOD'S INSTRUCTIONS ARE PERFECT

God's instructions are complete. They're not weak or partial. What God has said is perfect, and it restores the soul. When we try to live our life apart from bringing glory to God, we miss the purpose for our lives, and so our souls become sick and even die. But God's instructions are perfect; they restore the soul. David wrote, *"He restores my soul; He guides me in the paths of righteousness for His name's sake"* (Psalm 23:3).

You were created to bring glory to God. The manufacturer, God himself, knows perfectly how our lives should work. So he has provided a set of instructions that will make sure that it all fits together as it was meant to. What God says is perfect, so let's be diligent in listening to what he says.

GOD'S INSTRUCTIONS ARE TRUSTWORTHY

You can trust what God says. His instructions are trustworthy, since he knows and loves us perfectly. The balance between God's knowledge and love is the reason why we can trust his instructions for life. If a person has all knowledge of you or me but is not motivated by love, there is potential for trouble, or even exploitation. But God is not like that. His knowledge of you is complete, but you can trust what he says because he is love. You and I can rest in his instructions because they are trustworthy.

The Glory of God

The Psalmist wrote,

The Lord leads with unfailing love and faithfulness
all who keep his covenant and obey his demands.
For the honor of your name, O Lord,
forgive my many, many sins.
Who are those who fear the Lord?
He will show them the path they should choose.
They will live in prosperity,
and their children will inherit the land.
The Lord is a friend to those who fear him.
He teaches them his covenant.
My eyes are always on the Lord,
for he rescues me from the traps of my enemies.

—Psalm 25:10-15, NLT

The old hymn says it best:

He giveth more grace as the burdens grow greater,
He sendeth more strength as the labours increase.
To added affliction, He added His mercy,
to multiplied trials—His multiplied peace.

When we have exhausted our store of endurance,
when our strength has failed ere the day is half done,
when we reach the end of our hoarded resources,
Our Father's full giving is only begun.

His love has no limits, His grace has no measure,
His power no boundary known to men.
And out of His infinite riches In Jesus,
He giveth, and giveth, and giveth again.[7]

God's help through his instructions brings wisdom!

GOD'S INSTRUCTIONS ARE RIGHT

God's instructions aren't meant to stifle fun and enjoyment. They are right! What God says is the right thing to do. His instructions for this life are fair. Someone may receive a gift at Christmas that needs to be assembled. If you're like me, when you finish putting the bookshelf or toy or whatever it is together it's very satisfying, and you feel a little bit of joy and accomplishment.

I remember assembling a cabinet for Carole. I wanted to dance around the room when it was complete and all the pieces were used! That's the way it is when we follow God's instructions for our lives. When he has completed his work in us, we rejoice because his instructions are right!

GOD'S INSTRUCTIONS ARE PURE

There is no impure motive in God's instructions. What God says gives understanding.

---

7   "He Giveth More Grace," Annie J. Flint, Public Domain

The Glory of God

When you and I look into what God has said and we finally have that "aha!" moment, we glorify him and are amazed at who he is. God does not send us hidden messages. His instructions are obvious because he has made them known.

The prophet Micah wrote, "...O people, the Lord has told you what is good, and this is what he requires of you: to do what is right, to love mercy, and to walk humbly with your God" (Micah 6:8).

We don't have to worry that when we finally stand before God, we will have somehow missed something he expected from us. God's instructions are pure, and we know deep down inside when we have sinned and come short of his glory. Remember: when our lives bring glory to God, we are living as we were created to be.

So what are God's instructions? Are they simply the Ten Commandments? God's instructions go much deeper than laws and regulations. God's instructions lead us to live for his glory. In other words, when we are living this way we love, we show patience, we are kind and forgiving, and we humbly serve others as a fragrant offering of worship to the one who is worthy of all praise.

When we lived in sin, we worshiped ourselves—defeating the purpose for which we were created. You and I are truly alive only when we are bringing glory and honor to our wonderful Savior.

God is awesome and amazing! His love and patience go beyond our mental ability to grasp. The only time we have a hint of the greatness of God's love and patience is when we—his creations—live as we were created to be.

A frail black woman stands slowly to her feet. She is about 70 years of age. Facing her from across the room are several white police officers, one of whom, Mr. Van der Broek, has just been tried and found implicated in the murders of both the woman's son and her husband some years before.

It was indeed Mr. Van der Broek, it has now been established, who had come to the woman's home a number of years back, taken her son, shot him at point-blank range and then burned the young man's body on a fire while he and his officers partied nearby.

Several years later, Van der Broek and his security police colleagues had returned to take away her husband as well. For many months she heard nothing of his whereabouts. Then, almost two years after her husband's disappearance, Van der Broek came back to fetch the woman herself. How vividly she remembers that evening, going to a place beside a river where she was shown her husband, bound and beaten, but still strong in spirit, lying on a pile of wood. The last words she heard from his lips as the officers poured gasoline over his body and set him aflame were, "Father, forgive them."

And now the woman stands in the courtroom and listens to the confessions offered by Mr. Van der Broek. A member of South Africa's Truth and Reconciliation Commission turns to her and asks, "So, what do you want? How should justice be done to this man who has so brutally destroyed your family?" "I want three things," begins the old woman, calmly but confidently. "I want first to be taken to the place where my husband's body was burned so that I can gather up the dust and give his remains a decent burial."

She pauses, then continues. "My husband and son were my only family. I want, secondly, therefore, for Mr. Van der Broek to become my son. I would like for him to come twice a month to the ghetto and spend a day with me so that I can pour out on him whatever love I still have remaining within me."

"And, finally," she says, "I want a third thing. I would like Mr. Van der Broek to know that I offer him my forgiveness because Jesus Christ died to forgive. This was also the wish of my husband. And so, I would kindly ask someone to come to my side and lead me across the courtroom so that I can take Mr. Van der Broek in my arms, embrace him and let him know that he is truly forgiven."

As the court assistants come to lead the elderly woman across the room, Mr. Van der Broek, overwhelmed by what he has just heard, faints. And as he does, those in the courtroom, friends, family, neighbors—all victims of decades of oppression and injustice—begin to sing, softly, but assuredly, "Amazing grace, how sweet the sound, that saved a wretch like me." [8]

---

8 http://www.thesundayleader.lk/2013/12/01/emulating-south-african-truth-and-reconciliation-commission/

God was glorified in this woman because she showed the love of God. She demonstrated the mercy of God. She lived out the forgiveness of God, and she showed the glory of God.

God is glorified even in the difficult places of life. Yes, that's right. Even in the temporary troubles of life, God can be glorified. In contrast to that godly woman from South Africa, we have an example of the worst being, who did not live as he was created to be. Lucifer was created to be a worshiper. He was to be a beautiful servant who would bless his creator, but he wanted glory for himself, and so he became Satan. In fact, he tempted Jesus Christ to worship him, but only God is to be worshiped because he created all that is, and he has no equal.

As the Scriptures say, *"God opposes the proud but favors the humble"* (James 4:6, NLT). God is worthy of all praise, and we get to join with the angels and all of creation in worship of God. Do you want to know why you exist? It is so you can glorify God, to show just how wonderful he is. So no matter what we do, we do it for the glory of God. We love our wives for the glory of God. We love our children for the glory of God. We love our employers for the glory of God, and most importantly, we love our enemies for the glory of God.

Paul wrote that husbands are to love their wives just as Christ loved the church—and oh, how Jesus loves the church. We love our enemies because that's what brings glory to God, because people will see in us that God loved his enemies by giving the Son as a sacrifice for the cleansing of sins. Paul wrote, *". . .whatever you do, do all for the glory of God"* (I Corinthians 10:31, NLT). But there is a truth here that is even greater: God did what we could not do for ourselves.

The Glory of God

We could never do enough to earn salvation, but *"God so loved the world, that He gave His only begotten Son, that whoever believes in Him shall not perish, but have eternal life"* (John 3:16).

God not only gives all we need to live in the way for which we were created, but he also gives us the strength to always live for his glory. We can't take credit for loving others, because it is God's love that works in us. Oh, the greatness of God who actually helps us! That's why we say things like "Praise God" when someone compliments us. We know that it is by the goodness of God that we can do anything.

The Psalmist wrote *"May the words of my mouth and the meditation of my heart [everything I do] be pleasing to you, O Lord, my rock and my redeemer"* (Psalm 19:14, NLT). When we bring glory to God we are not appeasing an angry God. We are fulfilling our lives' purpose, which is to show the greatness of the Creator. He has no equal. He's greater than all of creation, and he has offered life to a rebellious and sinful world. Remember that the angel choir sang, *"Glory to God in the highest, and on earth peace among men with whom He is pleased"* (Luke 2:14). When we live for the glory of God, we are truly at peace—and best of all, we are pleasing our wonderful creator. That's what Christmas is all about.

chapter nine

THIS IS CHRIST

The angel told Mary,

> *...you will conceive in your womb and bear a son, and you shall name Him Jesus. He will be great and will be called the Son of the Most High; and the Lord God will give Him the throne of His father David; and He will reign over the house of Jacob forever, and His kingdom will have no end.*

—Luke 1:31-33

Before telling her this news, he said "don't be afraid." As we stated earlier, there are four main "fear nots" that set up the first Christmas.

The angel gave four reasons why Mary's fear could be dismissed. The angel said that the baby born to Mary would be great, that he would be called the Son of the Most High, that he would be given the throne of His father (descendant) David, and that he would reign forever.

DON'T BE AFRAID—HE IS GREAT (V. 32)

When we think of the first Christmas, we have warm feelings about that baby in the manger. However, let's also remember that thirty years later Jesus was rejected by this sinful world. He was accused of many things, including:

A keeper of bad company - Matthew 9:10-11
Of poor, common stock - Mark 6:3
A laborer - Mark 6:3
Demon-possessed - John 7:20, 8:48 and 52, 10:20,
Possessed of the devil himself - Mark 3:22
From the wrong neighborhood - John 7:41, 52
A deceiver and hypocrite - John 7:10-13
Unlearned - John 7:14-15
A false prophet - John 7:50-52
A liar - John 8:13
A bastard - John 8:19
A half-breed - John 8:48
A sinner - John 9:13-16
Crazy, insane - John 10:20
A blasphemer - John 10:31-33
Having a persecution complex - John 7:20
Provoking to anger - John 7:23
Sowing division among the people - John 7:43
Perplexing, causing doubt - John 10:22-24

But Jesus Christ is great. Awards are given for being the best singer, best hockey player, and best movie-maker, but Jesus Christ is truly great!

We read in Luke 7 that Jesus raised a dead man. People witnessing what happened said, *"God has visited His people"* (Luke 7:16). Jesus showed the love of God to the outcast and the sinner. He healed the blind and the chronically sick, and he provided for the needy. Not only does Jesus continue to heal, he also saves us and invites us to life in him. It's only through the wonderful gift of his own life that anyone has hope of life at all. He is not just the savior of the year, with someone due to surpass him next year. He is great, and will be great for all of eternity! Don't be afraid. He is great and you can trust him with your life.

DON'T BE AFRAID—HE IS THE SON OF THE MOST HIGH (V. 32)

The angel was right—Jesus is more than just a man who was born more than 2000 years ago.

He is known to be the Son of God. The term "Son of God" occurs forty-seven times in the New Testament.

In reference to Jesus, the title names him as the heavenly, eternal Son who is equal to God the Father (John 5:18-24). It is Jesus who fully reveals the Father (Matthew 11:27). He is the exact representation of the Father (Hebrews 1:1-3), he possesses all authority in heaven and earth (Matthew 28:18), and he shared the Father's glory before the world was made (John 17:5). He was not created; rather, he created all things. On that day in Bethlehem, the Son clothed himself in humanity. So "Son of God" is language used of Jesus not just in his humanity, but in his relationship with God the Father. And this relationship goes beyond a physical, biological one. We may say that someone is a son of a particular philosophy or school of thought. In sports, for example, a son of Peyton Manning would be a quarterback who models their style after this hall-of-fame football player. Additionally, my son, Jeremy Michael Telman, was not physically born to Carole and me. We had the joy of adopting him when he needed a mom and dad. Also, there is a pastor in Uganda that calls me Dad. I have never seen him in person, but I mentor and pray for him as a biological father would.

Make no mistake, the Son of God always has been, and always will be, God. He had no beginning and will have no end. At a time appointed by God the Father, he came to this earth and took on flesh. We use "son" as a word indicating a unique relationship.

Peter said to Jesus, *"You have words of eternal life. We believe and have come to know that You are the Holy One of God"* (John 6:68-69). Even the devil knew who Jesus was, and tempted Jesus to "prove himself": *"When the tempter came to him, he said, If thou be the Son of God, command that these stones be made bread"* (Matthew 4:3, KJV). Don't be afraid; Jesus Christ is the Son of the most high. You can trust him. You can place your faith in his love, goodness, and greatness.

DON'T BE AFRAID—HE IS ON THE THRONE (V. 32)

Most people worry and fear throughout their lives, but Jesus Christ sits on the throne of all Creation. As Stephen was being stoned, we read that he saw the Son of God stand up from his throne. When

Stephen was martyred he did not fear, but he forgave (Acts 7). Stephen knew who was truly on the throne: Jesus Christ!

Historically, David sat and ruled for 43 years. After him came Solomon, Rehoboam, and twenty-one other kings down to Zedekiah (587 B.C.); all occupied a literal throne in Jerusalem. Jesus said to Pilate,

> *"My kingdom is not of this world. If My kingdom were of this world, then My servants would be fighting so that I would not be handed over to the Jews; but as it is, My kingdom is not of this realm." Therefore Pilate said to Him, "So You are a king?" Jesus answered, "You say correctly that I am a king. For this I have been born, and for this I have come into the world, to testify to the truth."*

—John 18:36-37

The sad fact is that this world, created by Jesus, has told him, "We don't want you on the throne." In fact the crowds cried out, *"We have no king but Caesar"* (John 19:15). This world may be cruel, sinful, rebellious and dangerous—but don't be afraid, Jesus Christ is on the throne!

The Psalmist wrote, *"Righteousness and justice are the foundation of your throne. Unfailing love and truth walk before you as attendants. Happy are those who hear the joyful call to worship, for they will walk in the light of your presence, Lord"* (Psalm 89:14-15, NLT).

The writer to the Hebrews said,

> *Nothing in all creation is hidden from God. Everything is naked and exposed before his eyes, and he is the one to whom we are accountable.*

So then, since we have a great High Priest who has entered heaven, Jesus the Son of God, let us hold firmly to what we believe. This High Priest of ours understands our weaknesses, for he faced all of the same testings we do, yet he did not sin. So let us come boldly to the throne of our gracious God. There we will receive his mercy, and we will find grace to help us when we need it most.

—Hebrews 4:13-16, NLT

You can place your faith in him this day, and in doing so you can appeal to him for his benevolent love and kindness. Don't be afraid: place your trust and faith in Jesus Christ, who sits on the throne even now.

DON'T BE AFRAID—HE WILL REIGN FOREVER (V. 33)

The great joy of every Christian is not any past or present gift, but the future continual reign of Jesus Christ. We expectantly wait for the reign of Jesus Christ with the Psalmist, who wrote,

I will praise you, Lord, with all my heart;
    I will tell of all the marvelous things you have done.
I will be filled with joy because of you.
    I will sing praises to your name, O Most High.
My enemies retreated;
    they staggered and died when you appeared.
For you have judged in my favor;
    from your throne you have judged with fairness.

You have rebuked the nations and destroyed the wicked;
*   you have erased their names forever.*
The enemy is finished, in endless ruins;
*   the cities you uprooted are now forgotten.*
But the Lord reigns forever,
*   executing judgment from his throne.*
He will judge the world with justice
*   and rule the nations with fairness.*
The Lord is a shelter for the oppressed,
*   a refuge in times of trouble.*
Those who know your name trust in you,
*   for you, O Lord, do not abandon those who search for you.*
—Psalm 9:1-10, NLT

Handel wrote the beautiful oratorio, *The Messiah*, which includes the famous "Hallelujah Chorus" that is popular at Christmas. Can you say "forever and ever"? Don't be afraid, but place your faith and trust in Jesus Christ who will reign forever and ever.

No matter how this past year has gone, Jesus Christ is near, calling us all to a deep relationship with him as we eagerly wait for his physical and visible return to this earth. The words of the angel to Mary were proven to be absolutely correct. Jesus Christ is great, he is the Son of the Most High, he is on the throne, and he will reign forever. The challenge today for all humanity is, will we ignore and rebel against him or will we confess him as Lord and King of our lives?

chapter ten

WHAT A DREAM!

H ave you ever had a strange dream? Maybe it was something you ate the night before, or perhaps you had something on your mind before you went to sleep. Well, a righteous man named Joseph once had a really strange dream. In it, he had an angel speak to him about God's Christmas gift to humanity. He was told about the Messiah, the Savior of the world. What a dream! Joseph woke from his dream and remembered what the angel said. The angel said three things about the Messiah that are good news for all of us.

> . . .the birth of Jesus Christ was as follows: when His mother Mary
> had been betrothed to Joseph, before they came together she was found
> to be with child by the Holy Spirit. And Joseph her husband, being a
> righteous man and not wanting to disgrace her, planned to send her
> away secretly. But when he had considered this, behold, an angel of the
> Lord appeared to him in a dream, saying, "Joseph, son of David, do
> not be afraid to take Mary as your wife; for the Child who has been
> conceived in her is of the Holy Spirit. She will bear a Son; and you

shall call His name Jesus, for He will save His people from their sins."
Now all this took place to fulfill what was spoken by the Lord through
the prophet: "BEHOLD, THE VIRGIN SHALL BE WITH CHILD AND SHALL
BEAR A SON, AND THEY SHALL CALL HIS NAME IMMANUEL," which
translated means, "God with us." And Joseph awoke from his sleep
and did as the angel of the Lord commanded him, and took Mary as
his wife, but kept her a virgin until she gave birth to a Son; and he
called His name Jesus.

—Matthew 1:18-25

THE SON

Mary had a son. He was a real person. The historical fact is that he
was born: he was not a ghost or just an idea, a principle that some
false teachers propose. Jesus slept, he ate food, he taught, he prayed,
he healed, he preached, he bled, and he was killed. And most importantly, he rose by his own power (John 10:17-18), so there can be no
doubt that he is both 100% man and 100% God. The importance
of this to all humankind cannot be minimized.

The family tree of Jesus was given (Matt. 1:1-17) because
the gospel of Matthew was given for Jews. The Jews knew that the
Messiah was to be from a certain family tree, a fact that featured
in promises to two patriarchs. To Abraham, the promise was that
through one of his descendants the world would be blessed (Genesis 22:18), and to David this same promised descendant would
come (Psalm 89:4).

Jews needed, and still need, to know that Jesus Christ was the
promise given to David and Abraham. Non-Jews need to know this

too. Our minds may have a hard time understanding just who he is, but that doesn't change the fact that he was literally born, as was prophesied by Isaiah (7:14). In fact, by his being born, Jesus fulfilled over three hundred prophecies. Earlier we looked at just three of these prophecies. The chance that any man might fulfill eight prophecies is one in ten to the seventeenth power. That would be one chance in one hundred quadrillion to fulfill a mere eight prophecies, but Jesus fulfilled over three hundred.

The angel said that a very special Son would be born to Mary. As we hear the Christmas story and get the warm fuzzies when we see the nativity scene played out, we must remember that Jesus was literally born, and this becomes even more significant when we look ahead to the crucifixion and resurrection.

Athanasius was an early church father from the third century who refuted false teaching about Jesus. He said,

> [God] took to Himself a body, a human body even as our own. Nor did He will merely to become embodied or merely to appear; had that been so, He could have revealed His divine majesty in some other and better way. No, He took *our* body, and not only so, but He took it directly from a spotless, stainless virgin, without the agency of human father—a pure body, untainted by intercourse with man.[9]

---

9 http://www.copticchurch.net/topics/theology/incarnation_st_athanasius.pdf

Athanasius taught that salvation was at issue: only one who was fully human could atone for human sin, and only one who was fully divine could have the power to save us. It is vitally important to understand that at the appointed time, God the creator came to this earth and humbled himself to be born in the flesh. The angel said that Mary, the virgin, would bear a Son.

THE NAME OF JESUS

The angel said that Joseph would call him Jesus, and that's what he did. The name "Jesus" is Latin; in Hebrew it is *Yahshua,* which means "God is salvation."

Parents usually put much thought into the name they give their child. Carole and I named our son Jeremy because Jeremiah means "appointed by God," and we believe that God appointed him to be our son. Biblical names often have significance. Examples of this would be Esau ("hairy") and Korah ("bald"). Some babies were named because of an incident at their birth, or their names were based on some hope or prayer of the parent, as in Zechariah's name ("God has remembered"). Sometimes babies received the name of an everyday object, like Tamar ("palm tree"), and Tabitha ("gazelle"). Parents often named their children according to the time they were born; for example, Shaharaim ("dawn"), and Hodesh ("new moon"). The condition of the mother also frequently inspired a name: Leah ("exhausted") and Mahli ("sick").

Every time anyone says the name of Jesus, they are speaking the truth that "God is salvation." He even told his disciples that *"Whatever you ask in My name, that will I do, so that the Father may be glorified in the Son. If you ask Me anything in My name, I will do it"* (John 14:13-14). When we recognize that God is salvation and not condemnation, we move from disbelief to belief in his goodness and power over any situation. Speak the name of Jesus!

The Apostle Paul, who met Jesus on the Damascus road, wrote, *"God highly exalted Him, and bestowed on Him the name which is above every name, so that at the name of Jesus every knee will bow, of those who are in heaven and on earth and under the earth, and that every tongue will confess that Jesus Christ is Lord, to the glory of God the Father"* (Philippians 2:11).

Remember, *". . .God did not send the Son into the world to judge the world, but that the world might be saved through Him"* (John 3:17). His name, the name Joseph was told to give him, makes demons tremble.

THE NAME OF IMMANUEL

The angel said that others would call him Immanuel. Earlier we discussed how Immanuel literally means "God with us." This name tells us about Jesus' mission and nature. His mission was to come to a fallen world, lonely and dying in sin. His nature is that he can be with you even while he is with me. He is God almighty, able to be with all who call upon him. He's big—really big!

Studies suggest the universe could have triple the number of stars scientists previously calculated. If you're counting, the new estimate is 300,000,000,000,000,000,000,000 stars. The Psalmist wrote, *"He [God] counts the number of the stars; He gives names to all of them. Great is our Lord and abundant in strength; His understanding is infinite"* (Psalm 147:4-5). God is not like you and me. He is beyond our minds to understand. He is really big and amazing. He is "God with us"; nevertheless, many people feel very much alone.

An ad in a Kansas newspaper read, "I will listen to you talk for 30 minutes without comment for $5.00." Sounds like a hoax, doesn't it? But the person was serious. Did anybody call? You bet. It wasn't long before this individual was receiving ten to twenty calls a day. The pain of loneliness was so sharp that some were willing to try anything for a half hour of companionship. The good news is that God saw and heard our cry.

Jesus was known by this nickname, "Immanuel," "God with us." When demons encountered him, they recognized that God was in their presence, and said *"You are the Son of God!"* (Mark 3:11, Luke 4:41). Peter said, *"You are the Christ, the Son of the living God"* (Matt. 16:16-17). Martha said, *"I have believed that You are the Christ, the Son of God, even He who comes into the world"* (John 11:27). When people saw him, they said, "Immanuel, God is with us."

The Jews sang a song that celebrates the fact that God is close: *"God is our refuge and strength, a very present help in trouble"* (Psalm 46:1). Paul the apostle wrote, *"Rejoice in the Lord always; again I will say, rejoice! Let your gentle spirit be known to all men. The Lord is near"* (Philippians 4:4-5).

You may not see Jesus Christ in the flesh right now, but you can know that he is with you because he has promised to be with you by his Spirit. You are never alone!

No matter what trouble comes around the corner or how we might feel, God is with us. This should move us to trust him and to be careful to honor him with every choice we make. The writer to the Hebrews reminds us that Jesus himself said, *"Never will I leave you, never will I forsake you"* (Hebrews 13:5, NIV).

What a Dream!

Immanuel! God is with us! The one who created all things. The one who gave himself for us. The one who heals. The one who is returning physically again is with us by his Spirit. The Psalmist wrote,

Where can I go from Your Spirit?
Or where can I flee from Your presence?
If I ascend to heaven, You are there;
If I make my bed in Sheol, behold, You are there.
If I take the wings of the dawn,
If I dwell in the remotest part of the sea,
Even there Your hand will lead me,
And Your right hand will lay hold of me.

—Psalm 139:7-10

God is big and we can't run away from him, but why would we want to? God is near to all who call out to him. We don't live by dreams and visions, but by the word of God. Joseph's dream was authentic because the coming of the Son of God was prophesied. Isn't it great to know that God writes history in advance? Our response to Jesus Christ is to remember that he came, he died, and he rose because we were in great need. Like Adam and Eve, we went our own ways. In essence, all of us, through our decisions, have said "God, leave me alone." God calls that sin.

We were created to have fellowship with God, but sin creates a huge cavernous void. Even so, Jesus came so that we could be saved from a life of emptiness and ultimate destruction. Call out to him today! Surrender your life to him right now and walk with him in a relationship that is greater than anything in this world.

chapter eleven

FROM RICHES TO RAGS

The Bible is not a self-help book; rather, it's the story of God and his love for you and all of creation. Without a doubt, Jesus is the most important figure in world history. More has been written about him, spoken about him, and considered about him than any other person in all of recorded human history. It has been said, in fact, that history is "His Story." Although he wrote no books and never traveled more than ninety miles from the place of his birth, Christianity is founded upon the life, teachings, and personal claims of Jesus of Nazareth. He remains the most controversial of history's notable characters. It's obvious that Jesus has a long list of enemies, past and present, yet one hundred million followers in China alone call him Savior. Who is Jesus? The Bible makes it clear through prophecy and through the experience of many that he is truly God clothed in flesh.

His throne was above all, but he came and was wrapped in "swaddling clothes," which literally means he was clothed in strips of cloth. He was laid in a feed trough, not a nicely padded crib. He went from Riches to Rags. We know the story of his humble birth, but let's read more about the one who loved us so much that left the riches of his throne to come and give himself as a sacrifice for you and me.

We usually think of someone rising to power or coming from Rags to Riches, but Jesus Christ did the opposite. He humbled himself by leaving his riches to walk with us and give himself for us. He divested himself of his glory and covered himself with human flesh.

The wealthy of the first century had little to do with Jesus. They rejected him. His low estate reached a climax when he was tried and crucified. He was forsaken even by what few friends he had. He was crucified between two thieves, and buried in a borrowed tomb. He took on human weakness, human limitations, human propensity to temptation, human loneliness and humiliation. He came into this foul world from the purity and glory of heaven. He was rejected, beaten, crucified and gave up his life because of love for you. He went from Riches to Rags.

Let's consider the riches of God in Christ Jesus.

HE WAS RICH, BUT BECAME POOR

For you know the grace of our Lord Jesus Christ, that though He was rich, yet for your sake He became poor, so that you through His poverty might become rich.

—2 Corinthians 8:9

In the 1800s, the author Horatio Alger coined the phrase "from rags to riches."[10] Alger was a wealthy man who devoted much of his time and money to helping orphans and runaway boys in New York City.

We all love a good "rags to riches" story don't we? We love to hear how a local boy who grew up in poverty made good through hard work and struggled and fought his way to the top. It does our hearts good to hear such stories. It may be that we like them since they give us hope that our situations can improve. But Jesus, who was rich, did exactly the opposite: he became poor.

Jesus Christ, the Son of God, who was immeasurably rich, became poor for us, who were lost in sin and bound by our spiritual debt. There was no way for us to pay the debt we owed for even a single sin. We needed the help of one who could do that and more, and so Jesus came from his throne.

In chapter two we introduced the Greek word *"charis,"* which simply means God's help and influence. It's by God's help and influence that we have life and the payment of our debt. So we place our faith in Jesus Christ and follow him. We do as he does. We love, give and care about others before ourselves.

We find Jesus' mission statement in the first message he preached in Nazareth, when he said (quoting Isaiah 61:1-2),

> *The Spirit of the Lord is on me, because he has anointed me to proclaim good news to the poor. He has sent me to proclaim freedom for the prisoners and recovery of sight for the blind, to set the oppressed*

---

10 https://en.wikipedia.org/wiki/Horatio_Alger,_Jr.

free, to proclaim the year of the Lord's favor. . . Today this scripture is fulfilled in your hearing.

—Luke 4:18-19, 21, NIV

He who was rich became poor that we might become rich. Later we will look at the riches that God offers to everyone. To say that Jesus was "rich" refers to his pre-existence as the Son of God. He enjoyed the presence of the Father and shared in his glory (John 17:5; I Timothy 3:16). But when he was born in Bethlehem, as was prophesied, he did not have any wealth to force people to follow him. It was his love for everyone that made the difference. We follow Jesus because he first loved us.

When you exchange gifts at Christmas, you hope to give something that is equal to the gift you receive. Let's face it: we feel uncomfortable when someone out-gives us. We may like receiving an extravagant gift, but then feel like we are indebted to the giver.

God made an exchange. He took on poverty so that we can live in abundance. If you're looking for abundance in things that will rust and eventually break, you will be disappointed. God gives more than the temporary. He gives us things that are more valuable than cars and toys.

GOD IS RICH IN KINDNESS AND GRACE

In Him we have redemption through His blood, the forgiveness of our trespasses, according to the riches of His grace. . .

—Ephesians I:7

From Riches to Rags

...in the ages to come He might show the surpassing riches of His grace in kindness toward us in Christ Jesus.

—Ephesians 2:7

Have you longed for kindness? Do you wish that people would just be kind to you? Kindness is something that God is rich in. You may know people who are poor in kindness—but God is rich in it.

In the 1930s, the millionaire John D. Rockefeller used to dress up in a suit and a top hat and have his picture taken giving some poor boy a dime. Now, while a dime was a lot of money in those days—it would be the equivalent of $2 or more today—the most that could be said of Rockefeller is that he was giving out of the abundance of his riches. However, if he had gone to one of those boys and had purchased for him a mansion in the country and given him a chauffeur-driven limousine, then it could be said that he was giving according to his riches.

That is the way God has saved us—not merely out of his riches, but according to his riches. How rich is God? How much grace does he possess? An inexhaustible supply. All of God's attributes are of infinite measure. So his kindness, his help, and his influence are ours if we will only possess them.

Sadly, many live in poverty when God is rich in kindness and grace. He forgives us our sins, and now we can forgive and love others because of the riches that we possess. If you struggle with forgiving and loving others, ask yourself "why?" You should submit to God and ask him to forgive you for not treating others the way he treats you.

GOD IS RICH IN MERCY (EPHESIANS 2:4)

God is not stingy or limited in mercy. You and I might struggle with being merciful, but God is rich in mercy. My good friend, Kerry Pocha, has often said that "We look for mercy but want judgment for others." Isn't that true?

Have you ever noticed the mistakes people make in traffic? If you're like me, you want them to get ticketed by the police—but when we break the law, we're looking for mercy. Have you ever had to go to the bank or a creditor and ask for mercy? Something happened and you couldn't make that month's payment. That has happened to me all too often. The problem with asking for mercy is that most of the time, creditors want your money more than they want to give mercy. But God is rich in mercy. He wants to pour his mercy on you. Will you accept it? He's compassionate towards us. We have earned judgment by sinning—but God, who is rich in mercy, gave the Son that the world might be saved and not condemned.

When asked about forgiveness and how often we are to forgive, Jesus told a parable about being in debt.

> Peter came and said to Him, "Lord, how often shall my brother sin against me and I forgive him? Up to seven times?" Jesus said to him, "I do not say to you, up to seven times, but up to seventy times seven.
>
> "For this reason the kingdom of heaven may be compared to a king who wished to settle accounts with his slaves. When he had begun to settle them, one who owed him ten thousand talents was brought to him. But since he did not have the means to repay, his lord commanded him to be sold, along with his wife and children and all that

he had, and repayment to be made. So the slave fell to the ground and prostrated himself before him, saying, 'Have patience with me and I will repay you everything.' And the lord of that slave felt compassion and released him and forgave him the debt. But that slave went out and found one of his fellow slaves who owed him a hundred denarii; and he seized him and began to choke him, saying, 'Pay back what you owe.' So his fellow slave fell to the ground and began to plead with him, saying, 'Have patience with me and I will repay you.' But he was unwilling and went and threw him in prison until he should pay back what was owed. So when his fellow slaves saw what had happened, they were deeply grieved and came and reported to their lord all that had happened. Then summoning him, his lord said to him, 'You wicked slave, I forgave you all that debt because you pleaded with me. Should you not also have had mercy on your fellow slave, in the same way that I had mercy on you?' And his lord, moved with anger, handed him over to the torturers until he should repay all that was owed him. My heavenly Father will also do the same to you, if each of you does not forgive his brother from your heart."

—Matthew 18:21-35

Jesus taught that the kingdom of God is all about mercy. You never have permission not to be merciful, no matter how bad things are. The point Jesus was making in this parable is that we owe God much more than people owe us. It goes against our every inclination and even our culture to do so, but we must be people of great mercy. This is where the rubber meets the road. Do we say we are followers of Jesus? Prove it by being merciful. God, in Jesus Christ, has shared with us the riches of his mercy so we can be merciful. If we resist, in fact, Jesus said that the forgiveness we ourselves need will be blocked.

Once there lived in a little village a doctor noted for his kindness and charity. After his death they found written across many of his accounts the notation: "Forgiven—too poor to pay." His widow objected and sued the people for payment. But the judge asked, "Is this your husband's signature?" "Yes," she replied. "Then," said the judge, "there is not a court in the land who can order a collection of the accounts where the doctor has written 'Forgiven.'"

The Bible is an economics book. It's all about wealth—or the lack of it. The Bible does not recognize wealth in terms of temporal possessions. The Bible reminds us that Satan comes to steal, and that God is the giver of all that is good. The Bible is clear that a follower of Jesus cannot also serve the "master" of material wealth.

Some translations have 2 Corinthians 5:21 stating that Jesus became sin, but a more accurate reading of the Greek is that Jesus came as the sin offering. Even our songs do not quite capture this nuance. Jesus did not become sin; he became the sin offering for you and me. He came as the payment. Only the sinless Son of God could qualify.

He went from Riches to Rags in order to serve as the payment for us. When Jesus gave himself up on the cross, our debt was canceled. To stay in a debtor's prison is foolish. Walk now in the riches of Jesus' love by following him. He came from Riches to Rags, all because he loves you. Respond to that love by giving back the one thing that he asks of you: your life. Surrender to him, not just now but every day. Let him live in you.

Conclusion

The day after Halloween, many businesses bring out their Christmas decorations. By December 25th, one might feel Christmas/holiday fatigue, especially when the season seems so shallow.

Over a lifetime, we being to approach the season with certain practices and traditions. Gifts are bought early so those that need to be sent a long distance arrive before Christmas Day. Other gifts decorate the bottom of the Christmas tree. On American Thanksgiving, my son Jeremy and I used to hang lights on the house. For years, my parents would send us a Dutch treat: chocolate letters (for Jeremy and me it was a J, and for Carole it was a C).

To get through the next four to six weeks with sanity intact, one either dives directly into the pressure to spend, or ignores all the hype. Most don't handle this well. Sadly, many people will not understand and celebrate what Christmas is truly about. We could talk about the secularization of Western culture, and it would be true that the Christ child has been replaced by Santa Claus, but that would be like cursing the darkness and expecting light. We all know that when we walk into a dark room, we simply need to flip the electric switch. "Flipping the switch" with regard to Christmas means talking about Jesus Christ. He's the light of the world. He is the one who lights our way.

By December 21st, the daylight has become its shortest. Darkness dominates. This can bring depression and gloom. Similarly, the replacing of Christmas with an artificial emphasis on the temporal, which inevitably avoids the true Christmas, makes the season dark. But as we have seen in these chapters, Christmas can be a joyous time of celebrating the light of the world. My hope and prayer is that you have seen Jesus in all of his glory throughout this book.

Christmas is on the calendar each year, but it is much more than December 25th and a few days off from work. Christmas is something we celebrate all year round. God, in Christ Jesus, came to this world of hate, danger, and death in order to show the Father's love. Not only did he come to teach us, he came to give his life so that we might receive cleansing from our sin. God loves us that much. Look past all the trappings of the holiday season and see Jesus. Invite him into your life, not only as your friend, but also as your Lord and Master. Christmas will reveal its most wonderful meaning to you.

Other books by John W. Telman

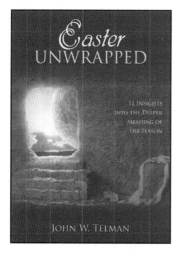

Life is so much more than merely the physical. You are more than a body. *Easter Unwrapped* presents 11 insights into just how significant the resurrection of Jesus is to everyone. When life hits you between the eyes, when you feel the darkness of death around, when you're faced with trouble that drains the life out of you, remember resurrection Sunday. It was the day that changed everything and it's more than chocolate and bunny rabbits. It's about life.

ISBN: 978-1-4866-1243-7
Retail Price: $12.99

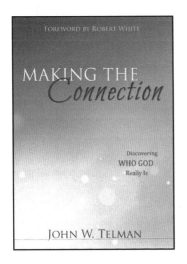

It is a sad fact that most people who do not believe in God have either an incomplete or false understanding of who the Almighty God is. This book, while valuable for such people, is not intended to be an apologetic, nor a defence. Simply, between the covers of this book is one man's observations of God, who has made himself known.

It's more than eternal life that is at stake. It's fellowship with God. Life without the creator is empty; plastic and worthless. It has no meaning. Fellowship with God is more than knowing facts about God. It is life based on who God is. When anyone has relationship with God, they truly live.

ISBN: 978-1-4866-0488-3
Retail Price: $12.99